Quick Colourful Quilts
for Beautiful Beds

Quick Colourful Quilts
for
Beautiful Beds

Edited by

Rosemary Wilkinson

NH
NEW HOLLAND

First published in 2006 by
New Holland Publishers (UK) Ltd
London I Cape Town I Sydney I Auckland
www.newhollandpublishers.com

Garfield House, 86-88 Edgware Road, London W2 2EA

80 McKenzie Street, Cape Town 8001, South Africa

Unit 4, 14 Aquatic Drive, Frenchs Forest, NSW 2086, Australia

218 Lake Road, Northcote, Auckland, New Zealand

10 9 8 7 6 5 4 3 2 1

ISBN 1 84537 455 X

Copy Editor: Patsy North
Design: Frances de Rees
Production: Hazel Kirkman
Photographs: Shona Wood
Illustrations: Carrie Hill
Template diagrams: Stephen Dew

Reproduction by Pica Digital PTE Ltd, Singapore
Printed and bound in Malaysia by
Times Offset (M) Sdn Bhd

NOTE
The measurements for each project are given in imperial and metric. Use only
one set of measurements – do not interchange them because they are not
direct equivalents.

CONTENTS

Basic Tools and Techniques

MATERIALS

PATCHWORK FABRICS

The easiest fabrics to work with for patchwork are closely woven, 100% cotton. They "cling" together making a stable unit for cutting and stitching, they don't fray too readily and they press well. Quilting shops and suppliers stock a fantastic range in both solid colours and prints, usually in 45 in/115 cm widths, and all of the quilts in this book are made using these cottons.

BACKING AND BINDING FABRICS

The backing and binding fabrics should be the same type and weight as the fabrics used in the patchwork top. They can be a coordinating colour or a strong contrast. You could also be adventurous and piece the backing, too, to make a reversible quilt. In either case, the colour of the binding needs to work with both the top and the backing fabric designs.

WADDING

Various types of wadding are available in cotton, polyester, wool or mixed fibres. They can be bought in pre-cut sizes suitable for the different sizes of bed quilts or in specific lengths cut from a bolt. They also come in different weights or "lofts" depending on how padded you want the quilt to be. Lightweight polyester wadding is the most commonly used, but some wool or cotton types are more suited to hand quilting. Some need to be closely quilted to prevent them from bunching up; others can be quilted up to 8 in/20 cm apart. If in doubt, follow the manufacturer's instructions.

QUANTITIES

The quantities given at the beginning of each project have been calculated to allow for a bit extra – just in case! A few of the quilts combine cutting down the length of the fabric with cutting across the width. This is to make the most economical use of fabric or to obtain border pieces cut in one piece.

Unless otherwise stated, any 10 in/25 cm requirement is the "long" quarter – the full width of the fabric – and not the "fat" quarter, which is a piece 18 x 22 in/50 x 56 cm.

PREPARATION

All fabrics should be washed prior to use in order to wash out any excess dye and to avoid fabrics shrinking at different rates. Wash each fabric separately and rinse – repeatedly if necessary – until the water is clear of any colour run. (If washing in a machine, cut a piece of white fabric from a larger piece. Place one piece in with the wash. After the wash, compare the white fabric with its other half. If they are the same, the fabric did not run. If a particular fabric continues to colour the water no matter how many times it is washed/rinsed and you have your heart set on using it, try washing it together with a small piece of each of the fabrics you intend to use with it. If these fabrics retain their original colours, i.e. they match the pieces not washed with the offending fabric, you would probably be safe in using it. But if in doubt – don't!

Once washed and before they are completely dry, iron the fabrics and fold them selvage to selvage – as they were originally on the bolt – in preparation for cutting. Be sure to fold them straight so that the selvages line up evenly, even if the cut edges are not parallel (this will be fixed later).

THREADS

For machine quilting use lightweight or monofilament threads. For quilting by hand, use a thread labelled "quilting thread", which is heavier than normal sewing thread. Some threads are 100% cotton; others have a polyester core that is wrapped with cotton. You can use a thread either to match or to contrast with the fabric that is being quilted. Alternatively, use a variegated thread toning or contrasting with the patchwork. It is also acceptable to use several colours on the same piece of work. If the quilt is to be tied rather than quilted, use a heavier thread, such as perle cotton, coton à broder or stranded embroidery cotton.

EQUIPMENT

There are some essential pieces of equipment that have revolutionized the making of patchwork quilts. Rotary cutting equipment, consisting of a rotary cutter used with an acrylic ruler and self-healing cutting mat, has speeded up the process of cutting shapes and made it more accurate; the sewing machine makes assembling the patchwork and quilting the finished piece quick and easy.

SEWING MACHINES

Evermore sophisticated, computerized machines are now available, but even a machine with just a straight stitch will speed up the process of assembling and quilting the patchwork considerably. Most sewing machines have a swing needle that allows the zig-zag stitching used for securing appliqué patches. Machines with decorative stitches provide the opportunity for additional embellishments.

LONGARM QUILTING MACHINES

These machines are used by professional quilters. You can choose from a huge library of quilting designs. There is also the option to have edge-to-edge quilting, all-over quilting of one design over the entire quilt, or a combination of patterns to complement each other. Alternatively, you can specify your own freehand style.

One of the advantages of this machine is that the quilt sandwich does not need to be tacked or pinned together prior to quilting: the pieced top, wadding and backing are mounted onto separate rollers that are part of the frame of the machine.

The machine is hand operated and takes considerable skill to work successfully. Most of the quilters who offer this quilting service advertise in patchwork magazines.

Below: bundles of fat quarters in co-ordinating colours are a great starting point for a patchwork colour scheme.

ROTARY CUTTING

Rotary cutting has become the most commonly used method of cutting fabrics for patchwork. Most rotary cutting tools are available with either imperial or metric measurements.

Rotary Cutters

There are several different makes available, mainly in three different sizes: small, medium and large. The medium size (45 mm) is probably the one most widely used and perhaps the easiest to control. The smallest can be difficult to use with rulers. The largest is very useful when cutting through several layers of fabric but can take some practice to use. The rotary blade is extremely sharp, so be sure to observe the safety instructions given on page 8. It does become blunted with frequent use, so it is worth always having a spare.

Rotary Rulers

Various different rulers are available for use with rotary cutters. These are made of acrylic and are sufficiently thick to act as a guide for the rotary blade. You must use these rulers with the

rotary cutter. Do not use metal rulers, as they will severely damage the blades.

The rulers are marked with measurements and angled lines to use as a guide when cutting the fabrics. Ideally, these markings should be on the underside of the ruler, laser printed and easy to read. Angles should be marked in both directions. Different makes of rulers can have the lines printed in different colours. Choose one that you find easy on your eyes. Some makes also have a non-slip surface on the back, which is helpful.

The two most useful rulers are either a 24 x 6 in/60 x 15 cm, or one that is slightly shorter, and the small bias square ruler, 6½ in or 15 cm. This ruler is particularly useful for marking squares containing two triangles – the half-square triangle units. There are many other rulers designed for specific jobs that you can purchase if and when needed.

Self-healing Rotary Cutting Mats

These are essential companions to the rotary cutter and ruler. Do not attempt to cut on any other surface. The mats come in a range of sizes and several different colours. The smaller ones are useful to take to classes, but for use at home, purchase the largest that you can afford and that suits your own workstation. There is usually a grid on one side, although both sides can be used. The lines on the mat are not always accurate, so it's better to use the lines on the ruler if possible.

OTHER USEFUL EQUIPMENT

Most other pieces of equipment are those that you will already have in your workbox. Those listed below are essential, but there is also a vast array of special tools devised by experienced quiltmakers that have specific uses. They are not needed by the beginner quilter but can really enhance the planning, cutting and quilting of your designs.

Scissors: Two pairs are needed. One large pair of good-quality scissors should be used exclusively for cutting fabric. The second, smaller pair is for cutting paper, card or template plastic.

Markers: Quilting designs can either be traced or drawn on the fabric prior to the layering or added after the layering with the aid of stencils or templates. Various marking tools are available: 2H pencils; silver, yellow or white pencils; fade away or washable marking pens; and Hera markers (which lightly indent the fabric). Whatever your choice, test the markers on a scrap of the fabric used in the quilt to ensure that the marks can be removed.

Pins: Good-quality, clean, rustproof, straight pins are essential when a pin is required to hold the work in place for piecing. Flat-headed flower pins are useful because they don't add bulk.

Safety pins: Special quilters' safety pins with curved sides are useful for holding the quilt "sandwich" together for quilting, especially for those who prefer to machine quilt or want the speed of not tacking/basting the three layers together.

Needles: For hand quilting, use "quilting" or "betweens" needles. Most quilters start with a no. 8 or 9 and progress to a no. 10 or 12. For machine stitching, the needles numbered 70/10 or 80/12 are both suitable for piecing and quilting. For making ties with thicker thread, use a crewel or embroidery needle.

Thimbles: Two thimbles will be required for hand quilting. One thimble is worn on the hand pushing the needle and the other on the hand underneath the quilt "receiving" the needle. There are various types on the market ranging from metal to plastic to leather sheaths for the finger. There are also little patches that stick to the finger to protect it.

HOOPS AND FRAMES

These are only needed if you are quilting by hand. They hold a section of the quilt under light tension to help you to achieve an even stitch. There are many types and sizes available, ranging from round and oval hoops to standing frames made of plastic pipes and wooden fixed frames.

Hoops are perhaps the easiest for a beginner. The 14 in/ 35 cm or 16 in/40 cm are best for portability. When the quilt is in the hoop, the surface of the quilt should not be taut, as is the case with embroidery. If you place the quilt top with its hoop on a table, you should be able to push the fabric in the centre of the hoop with your finger and touch the table beneath. Without this "give", you will not be able to "rock" the needle for the quilting stitch. Do not leave the quilt in a hoop when you are not working on it, as the hoop will distort the fabrics.

SAFETY

All rotary cutters have some form of safety mechanism that should always be used. Close the safety cover over the blade after every cut you make, whether or not you intend to continue with another cut. Safety habits are essential and will help prevent accidents. Ensure that the cutters are safely stored out of the reach of children.

Keep the cutter clean and free of fluff. An occasional drop of sewing machine oil helps it to rotate smoothly. Avoid running over pins, as this ruins the blade. Renew the blade as soon as it becomes blunt, as a blunt blade makes for inaccurate and difficult cutting and can damage the cutting mat. Replacement blades are readily available and there are also blade sharpening/exchange services.

TECHNIQUES

ROTARY CUTTING

The basis of rotary cutting is that fabric is cut first in strips – usually across the width of the fabric – then cross-cut into squares or rectangles. Unless otherwise stated, fabric is used folded selvage to selvage, wrong sides together, as it has come off the bolt.

MAKING THE EDGE STRAIGHT

Before any accurate cutting can be done, you must first make sure the cut edge of the fabric is at right angles to the selvages.

1 Place the folded fabric on the cutting mat with the fabric smoothed out, the selvages exactly aligned at the top and the bulk of the fabric on the side that is not your cutting hand. Place the ruler on the fabric next to the cut edge, aligning the horizontal lines on the ruler with the fold and with the selvages.

2 Place your non-cutting hand on the ruler to hold it straight and apply pressure. Keep the hand holding the ruler in line with the cutting hand. Place the cutter on the mat just below the fabric and up against the ruler. Start cutting by running the cutter upwards and right next to the edge of the ruler (diagram 1).

diagram 1

3 When the cutter becomes level with your extended fingertips, stop cutting but leave the cutter in position and carefully move the hand holding the ruler further along the ruler to keep the applied pressure in the area where the cutting is taking place. Continue cutting and moving the steadying hand as necessary until you have cut completely across the fabric. As soon as the cut is complete, close the safety shield on the cutter. If you run out of cutting mat, you will need to reposition the fabric, but this is not ideal as it can bring the fabric out of alignment.

4 Open out the narrow strip of fabric just cut off. Check to make sure that a "valley" or a "hill" has not appeared at the point of the fold on the edge just cut; it should be perfectly straight. If it is not, the fabric was not folded correctly. Fold the fabric again, making sure that this time the selvages are exactly aligned. Make another cut to straighten the edge and check again.

CUTTING STRIPS

The next stage is to cut strips across the width of the fabric. To do this, change the position of the fabric to the opposite side of the board, then use the measurements on the ruler to cut the strips, as follows:

1 Place the fabric on the cutting mat on the side of your cutting hand. Place the ruler on the mat so that it overlaps the fabric. Align the cut edge of the fabric with the vertical line on the ruler that corresponds to the measurement that you wish to cut. The horizontal lines on the ruler should be aligned with the folded edge and the selvage of the fabric.

2 As before, place one hand on the ruler to apply pressure while cutting the fabric with the other hand (diagram 2).

diagram 2

CROSS-CUTTING

The strips can now be cut into smaller units, described as cross-cutting, and these units are sometimes sub-cut into triangles.

Squares

1 Place the strip just cut on the cutting mat with the longest edge horizontal to you and most of the fabric on the side of the non-cutting hand. Cut off the selvages in the same way in which you straightened the fabric edge at the start of the process.

2 Now place the strip on the opposite side of the mat and cut

across (cross-cut) the strip using the same measurement on the ruler as used for cutting the strip; ensure that the horizontal lines of the ruler align with the horizontal edges of the fabric. You have now created two squares of the required measurement (diagram 3). Repeat as required.

diagram 3

Rectangles

1 First cut a strip to one of the required side measurements for the rectangle. Remove the selvages.

2 Turn the strip to the horizontal position as for the squares.

3 Cross-cut this strip using the other side measurement required for the rectangle. Again, ensure that the horizontal lines of the ruler align with the horizontal cut edges of the strip.

Multi-strip Units

This two-stage method of cutting strips, then cross-cutting into squares or rectangles, can also be used to speed up the cutting of multi-strip units to provide strip blocks, such as those used for the City Slicker quilt on page 18.

1 Cut the required number and size of strips and stitch together as per the instructions for the block/quilt you are making. Press the seams and check that they are smooth on the right side of the strip unit with no pleats or wrinkles.

2 Place the unit right side up in the horizontal position on the cutting mat. Align the horizontal lines on the ruler with the longer cut edges of the strips and with the seam lines just created (diagram 4). If, after you have cut a few cross-cuts, the lines on the ruler do not line up with the cut edges as well as the seam lines, re-cut the end to straighten it before cutting any more units.

diagram 4

ROTARY CUTTING TRIANGLES

Squares can be divided into either two or four triangles, called half-square or quarter-square triangles. Both sizes of triangle can be quickly cut using the rotary cutter or they can be made even faster by a quick piecing method described on pages 11 and 12.

Cutting Half-square Triangles

1 Cut the fabric into strips of the correct depth and remove the selvages.

2 Cross-cut the strips into squares of the correct width.

3 Align the 45° angle line on the ruler with the sides of the square and place the edge of the ruler so that it goes diagonally across the square from corner to corner. Cut the square on this diagonal, creating two half-square triangles.

Cutting Quarter-square Triangles

1 Cut the fabric into strips of the correct depth and remove the selvages.

2 Cross-cut the strips into squares of the correct width.

3 Cut the square into two half-square triangles, as above.

4 You can either repeat this procedure on the other diagonal or, if you are wary of the fabric slipping now that it is in two pieces, separate the two triangles and cut them individually. Align one of the horizontal lines of the ruler with the long edge of the triangle, the 45° line with the short edge of the triangle and the edge of the ruler placed on the point of the triangle opposite the long edge. Cut this half-square triangle into two quarter-square triangles.

SEAMS

To stitch accurately, you must be able to use the correct seam allowance without having to mark it on the fabric. To do this, you use either the foot or the bed of your sewing machine as a guide. Many machines have a "¼ in" or "patchwork" foot available as an extra. Before you start any piecing, check that you can stitch this seam allowance accurately.

Checking the Machine for the Correct Seam Allowance

Unthread the machine. Place a piece of paper under the presser foot, so that the right-hand edge of the paper aligns with the right-hand edge of the presser foot. Stitch a seam line on the paper. A row of holes will appear. Remove the paper from the machine and measure the distance from the holes to the edge of the paper. If it is not the correct width, i.e. ¼ in/0.75 cm, try one of the following:

1 If your machine has a number of different needle positions, try moving the needle in the direction required to make the seam allowance accurate. Try the test of stitching a row of holes again.

2 Draw a line on the paper to the correct seam allowance, i.e. ¼ in/0.75 cm from the edge of the paper. Place the paper under the presser foot, aligning the drawn line with the needle. Lower the presser foot to hold the paper securely and, to double-check, lower the needle to ensure that it is directly on top of the drawn line.

Fix a piece of masking tape on the bed of the machine so that the left-hand edge of the tape lines up with the right-hand edge of the paper. This can also be done with magnetic strips available on the market to be used as seam guides. But do take advice on using these if your machine is computerized or electronic.

Stitching ¼ in/0.75 cm Seams

When stitching pieces together, line up the edge of the fabric with the right-hand edge of the presser foot or with the left-hand edge of the tape or the magnetic strip on the bed of your machine, if you have used this method.

Checking the Fabric for the Correct Seam Allowance

As so much of the success of a patchwork depends on accuracy of cutting and seaming, it is worth double-checking on the fabric that you are stitching a ¼ in/0.75 cm seam.

Cut three strips of fabric 1½ in/4 cm wide. Stitch these together along the long edges to make a multi-strip unit of three pieces. Press the seams away from the centre strip. Measure the centre strip. It should measure exactly 1 in/2.5 cm wide. If not, reposition the needle/tape and try again.

Stitch Length

The stitch length used is normally 12 stitches to the inch or 5 to the centimetre. If the pieces being stitched together are to be cross-cut into smaller units, it is advisable to slightly shorten the stitch, which will mean the seam is less likely to unravel. It is also good practice to start each new project with a new needle in a clean machine – free of fluff around the bobbin housing.

QUICK MACHINE PIECING

The three most basic techniques are for stitching pairs of patches together (chain piecing), for stitching half-square triangle units and for stitching quarter-square triangle units.

Chain Piecing

Have all the pairs of patches or strips together ready in a pile. Place the first two patches or strips in the machine, right sides together, and stitch them together. Just before reaching the end, stop stitching and pick up the next two patches or strips. Place them on the bed of the machine, so that they just touch the patches under the needle. Stitch off one set and onto the next. Repeat this process until all the pairs are stitched to create a "chain" of pieced patches/strips (diagram 5). Cut the thread between each unit to separate them. Open out and press the seams according to the instructions given with each project.

diagram 5

Stitching Half-square Triangle Units

This is a quick method of creating a bi-coloured square without cutting the triangles first.

1 Cut two squares of different coloured fabrics to the correct measurement, i.e. the finished size of the bi-coloured square plus ⅝ in/1.75 cm. Place them right sides together, aligning all raw edges. On the wrong side of the top square, draw a diagonal line from one corner to the other (diagram 6).

diagram 6

2 Stitch ¼ in/0.75 cm away on either side of the drawn line, chain piecing the units to save time (diagram 7).

diagram 7

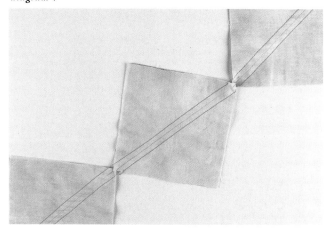

3 Cut along the drawn line to separate the two halves. Open out and press the seams according to the instructions given with each project. You now have two squares, each containing two triangles. Trim off the corners (diagram 8).

diagram 8

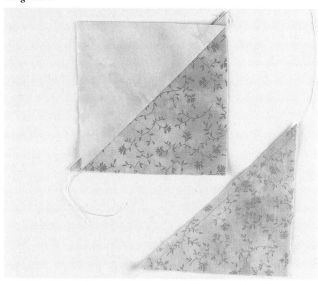

Stitching Quarter-square Triangle Units

This method also creates triangles from squares without first cutting the triangles.

1 Cut squares to the finished size of a square containing four triangles plus 1¼ in/3.5 cm. Follow the stitching, cutting apart and pressing sequence as for the half-square triangle units.

2 Place the two bi-coloured squares right sides together. Ensure that each triangle is facing a triangle of a different colour. Draw a line diagonally from corner to corner, at right angles to the stitched seam.

3 Pin carefully to match the seams, then stitch ¼ in/0.75 cm away on either side of the line. Before cutting apart, open up each side and check to see that the points match in the centre .

4 Cut apart on the drawn line. You now have two squares, each containing four triangles (diagram 9).

diagram 9

PRESSING

Each project will have instructions on the direction in which to press the seam allowances. These have been designed to facilitate piecing at junctions and to reduce the bulk so that seam allowances do not lie one on top of the other. Pressing as you complete each stage of the piecing will also improve the accuracy and look of your work. Take care not to distort the patches. Be gentle, not fierce, with the iron.

ADDING THE BORDERS

Most patchwork tops are framed by one or more borders. The simplest way of adding borders is to add strips first to the top and bottom of the quilt and then to the sides, producing abutted corners. A more complicated method is to add strips to adjacent sides and join them with seams at 45 degrees, giving mitred borders. Only the first method is used for the quilts in this book.

Adding Borders with Abutted Corners

The measurements for the borders required for each quilt in the book will be given in the instructions. However, it is always wise to measure your own work to determine the actual measurement.

1 Measure the quilt through the centre across the width edge to edge. Cut the strips for the top and bottom borders to this length by the width specified for the border.

2 Pin the strips to the quilt by pinning first at each end, then in the middle, then evenly spaced along the edge. By pinning in this manner, it is possible to ensure that the quilt "fits" the border. Stitch the border strips into position on the top and bottom edge of the quilt (diagram 10). Press the seams towards the border.

diagram 10

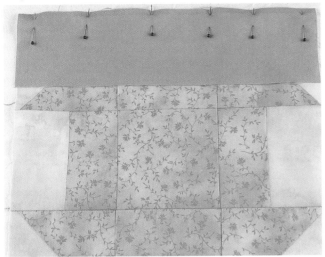

3 Measure the quilt through the centre from top to bottom. Cut the side border strips to this measurement.

4 Pin and stitch the borders to each side of the quilt as before (diagram 11). Press the seams towards the border.

diagram 11

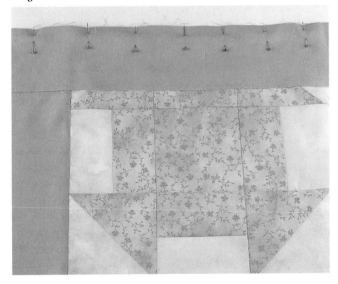

QUILTING

The three layers or "sandwich" of the backing/wadding/pieced top that make up a patchwork quilt are held together by quilting or by tying. The quilting can be done by hand or machine. The tying is done by hand-stitching decorative ties at strategic points on the quilt, as in All Churned Up on page 78.

Layering/Sandwiching

Prior to any quilting, unless you are using a longarm quilting machine (see page 7), the pieced top must be layered with the wadding and the backing. The wadding and the backing should be slightly larger than the quilt top – approximately 2 in/5 cm on all sides. There are two different methods for assembling the three layers, depending on whether the quilt has bound edges or not.

Assembling Prior to Binding

1 Lay out the backing fabric wrong side uppermost. Ensure that it is stretched out and smooth. Secure the edges with masking tape at intervals along the edges to help hold it in position.

2 Place the wadding on top of the backing fabric. If you need to join two pieces of wadding first, butt the edges and stitch together by hand using a herringbone stitch (diagram 12).

diagram 12

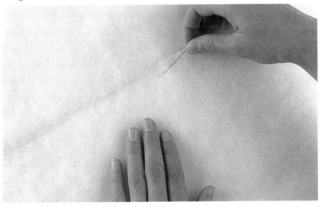

3 Place the pieced top right side up and centred on top of the wadding.

Assembling Where No Binding is Used – Called "Bagging Out"

1 Spread out the wadding on a flat surface. Smooth out to ensure there are no wrinkles.

2 Place the backing fabric centrally on top of the wadding, right side uppermost.

3 Place the pieced top centrally over the backing, wrong side uppermost. Pin with straight pins around the edges to keep them together.

4 Stitch around all four sides with a $^1/_4$ in/0.75 cm seam allowance but leaving an opening of about 15–18 in/35–45 cm in one of the sides.

5 Trim the excess wadding and backing at the sides and across the corners to reduce bulk, then turn the quilt right side out, so that the wadding is in the middle. Slip-stitch the opening closed.

6 Smooth out the layers of the quilt and roll and finger-press the edges so that the seam lies along the edge or just underneath.

Basting Prior to Quilting

If the piece is to be quilted rather than tied, the three layers now need to be held together at regular intervals. This can be done by basting or by using safety pins. For either method, start in the centre of the quilt and work out to the edges.

To baste the layers together, using a long length of thread, start basting in the centre of the quilt top. Only pull about half of the thread through as you start stitching. Once you have reached the edge, go back and thread the other end of the thread and baste to the opposite edge. Repeat this process, stitching in a grid of horizontal and vertical lines over the whole quilt top (diagram 13).

diagram 13

If using safety pins, place the pins at regular intervals all over the quilt surface (diagram 14)

diagram 14

MACHINE QUILTING

Designs to be used for machine quilting should ideally be those that have one continuous line. The lines can be straight or free-form curves and squiggles. For either type, be sure to keep the density of stitching the same. With either method, continuous lines of stitching will be visible both on the top and on the back of the quilt. It is a quick method but requires careful preparation.

There is a wide variety of tools available designed to help make handling the quilt easier during the machine quilting process. Some machines require a walking foot to stitch the three layers together. These are used with the feed dogs up and, while in use, the machine controls the direction and stitch length. However, the most essential requirement is practice.

It is worth making up a practice sandwich – if possible using the same fabrics and wadding as used in the actual quilt – to be

sure that you get the effect you want. In any case, plan the quilting design first, otherwise there is a danger that you will start with quite dense stitching, then tire of the process and begin to space out the lines, producing an uneven pattern.

When starting and stopping the stitching during machine quilting, either reduce the stitch length to zero or stitch several stitches in one spot. If you do not like the build-up of stitches that this method produces, leave long tails on the thread when you start and stop. Later, pull these threads through to one side of the quilt, knot them, then thread them into a needle. Push the needle into the fabric and into the wadding, but not through to the other side of the quilt, and then back out through the fabric again about 1 in/2.5 cm away from where the needle entered the quilt. Cut off the excess thread.

In-the-ditch Machine Quilting

One of the easiest and most common forms of straight line quilting is called "in-the-ditch" and involves stitching along a seam line where it is almost invisible (diagram 15). To do this, slightly part the fabric at the seam, then let it settle back after stitching.

diagram 15

Echo Quilting

This is also a popular type of straight line quilting where the quilting is stitched $^1/_4$ in/0.75 cm away from the shape or seam line (diagram 16).

diagram 16

Free Motion Machine Quilting

When machine quilting in freehand, a darning foot is used with the feed dogs down, so that you can move the quilt forwards, backwards and sideways. This is easier on some machines than others, but all require a bit of practice. The design shown here is called vermicelli (diagram 17).

diagram 17

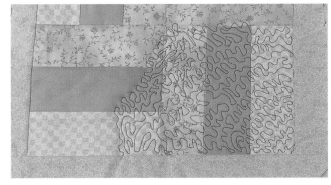

Hand Quilting

Place the section of the quilt to be worked on in a hoop as described on page 8. The stitch used for hand quilting is a running stitch. The needle goes into the quilt through to the back and returns to the top of the quilt all in one movement. The aim is to have the size of the stitches and spaces between them the same length.
1 Thread a needle with an 18 in/45 cm length of quilting thread and knot the end. Push the needle into the fabric and into the wadding, but not through to the back, about 1 in/2.5 cm away from where you want to start stitching. Bring the needle up through the fabric at the point where you will begin stitching. Gently pull on the thread to "pop" the knot through into the wadding.

2 To make a perfect quilting stitch, the needle needs to enter the fabric perpendicular to the quilt top. Holding the needle between your first finger and thumb, push the needle into the fabric until it hits the thimble on the finger of the hand underneath.
3 The needle can now be held between the thimble on your sewing hand and the thimble on the finger underneath. Release your thumb and first finger hold on the needle. Place your thumb on the quilt top just in front of where the needle will come back up to the top and gently press down on the quilt (diagram 18).

diagram 18

4 At the same time, rock the thread end of the needle down towards the quilt top and push the needle up from underneath so that the point appears on the top of the quilt. You can either pull the needle through now, making only one stitch, or rock the needle up to the vertical again, push the needle through to the back, then rock the needle up to the quilt top, again placing another stitch on the needle. Repeat until you can no longer rock the needle into a completely upright position (diagram 19). Pull the needle through the quilt. One stitch at a time, or several placed on the needle at once – "the rocking stitch" – before pulling the thread through, are both acceptable.

diagram 19

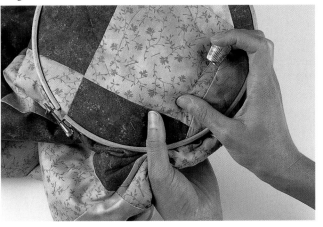

5 When the stitching is complete, tie a knot in the thread close to the quilt surface. Push the needle into the quilt top and the wadding next to the knot, but not through to the back of the quilt. Bring the needle up again about 1 in/2.5 cm away and gently tug on the thread to "pop" the knot through the fabric and into the wadding. Cut the thread close to the surface.

BINDING

Once the quilting is completed, the quilt is usually (but not always) finished off with a binding to enclose the raw edges. This binding can be cut on the straight or on the bias. Either way, the binding is usually best done with a double fold. It can be applied in four separate pieces to each of the four sides, or the binding strips can be joined together and stitched to the quilt in one continuous strip with mitred corners. To join straight-cut pieces for a continuous strip, use straight seams; to join bias-cut pieces, use diagonal seams (diagram 20).

diagram 20

For either method, the width of the bias strips should be cut to the following measurement: finished binding width x four + the seam allowance x two.

For example:

A finished binding width of $\frac{1}{2}$ in would be cut as $2\frac{1}{2}$ in:

$(\frac{1}{2}$ in x 4$) + (\frac{1}{4}$ in x 2$) = 2\frac{1}{2}$ in

or 1.25 cm would be cut 6.5 cm:

$(1.25$ cm x 4$) + (0.75$ cm x 2$) = 6.5$ cm

Continuous Strip Binding

1 Fold the binding in half lengthwise with wrong sides together and lightly press.

2 Place the raw edges of the binding to the raw edge of the quilt – somewhere along one side, not at a corner. Commence stitching about 1 in/2.5 cm from the end of the binding and, using the specified seam allowance, stitch the binding to the quilt through all layers of the "sandwich" (diagram 21). Stop $\frac{1}{4}$ in/ 0.75 cm from the end. At this point, backstitch to secure, then break off the threads. Remove the quilt from the sewing machine.

3 Place the quilt on a flat surface, with the binding just stitched at the top edge; fold the binding up and away from the quilt to "twelve o'clock", creating a 45° fold at the corner (diagram 22).

diagram 21

diagram 22

4 Fold the binding back down to "six o'clock", aligning the raw edges of the binding to the raw edge of the quilt. The fold created on the binding at the top should be the same distance away from the seam as the width of the finished binding (diagram 23).

diagram 23

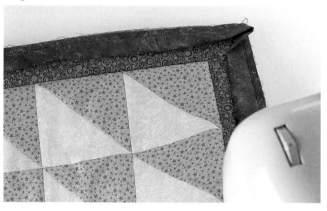

5 Start stitching the binding to the quilt at the same point where the previous stitching stopped. Secure with backstitching, then continue to the next corner. Repeat the process at each corner.

6 Stop about 2 in/5 cm from where you started. Open out the fold on both ends of the binding, then seam the two ends together. Trim away the excess, refold and finish applying the binding to the quilt.

7 Trim the excess wadding and backing fabric so that the distance from the stitching line equals or is slightly wider than that of the finished binding. Fold the binding over to the back and hand stitch the folded edge of the binding to the quilt along the row of machine stitching just created. A mitre will appear at the corners on the front and on the back of the binding. Slip-stitch these in place.

Binding the Four Sides Separately

1 Cut binding strips to the required width. Fold in half lengthwise with wrong sides together and lightly press.

2 Measure the pieced top through the centre from top to bottom and cut two of the binding strips to this length.

3 Pin one of the strips down the side of the quilt, right sides together and aligning raw edges. Stitch with the usual seam allowance. Trim the excess wadding and backing fabric so that the distance from the stitching line equals or is slightly wider than that of the finished binding (diagram 24).

diagram 24

4 Fold the binding strip to the back of the quilt and slip stitch to the backing fabric. Trim the ends level with the wadding. Do the same on the opposite side of the quilt with the other strip.

5 Measure the quilt through the centre from side to side and add 1 ½ in/4 cm for turnings. Cut two more binding strips to this length, joining if necessary. Stitch to the top and bottom of the quilt, leaving a ¾ in/2 cm overhang at each end. Trim the backing and wadding as above. Then turn in a short hem at either end before folding to the back and slip-stitching down. Slip-stitch the corners neatly.

HANGING SLEEVE

If your quilt is a wallhanging or is to be exhibited, it will need a hanging sleeve. A sleeve can be added after the quilt is completely finished, but a more secure and permanent sleeve can be added along with the binding.

1 Cut a piece of fabric, preferably matching the backing, to measure 10 in/25 cm deep by the width of the quilt. Make a 1 in/ 2.5 cm hem on both the short ends.

2 Fold the fabric in half along the length with wrong sides together. Centre this on the back of the quilt, aligning the raw edges of the sleeve with the raw edges of the quilt. Pin, then tack.

3 Turn the quilt over so the front is uppermost. Stitch the binding in the normal way, which will then secure the hanging sleeve at the same time (diagram 25).

4 Finish hand stitching on the binding.

5 Lay the quilt on a flat surface with the back uppermost. Smooth out the sleeve and pin the lower edge so that it rests evenly on the back of the quilt.

diagram 25

6 Stitch the sleeve to the back of the quilt along the fold at the bottom of the sleeve, then stitch the underneath edge at each short end, so that when a rod is inserted it will not actually touch the back of the quilt, only the sleeve fabric. Take care that your stitches only go into the back and wadding of the quilt and are not visible on the front. Remove the pins.

HINTS AND TIPS

Chain Piecing
To further speed up this process, place the two pieces/strips to be stitched together beside the sewing machine. Place one group of patches facing up and one group facing down. Now when you pick up one piece, its partner is in the correct position to place on top, right sides together.

Pressing Seams
Always press seams to one side unless otherwise stated, as an open seam is put under more strain. Press fabrics towards the darker fabric to prevent show-through.

Slip-stitched Seams
To finish the slip-stitched seam neatly (e.g. when bagging out a quilt), before you turn your quilt, stitch across the turning opening using the longest stitch your machine will make. Finger-press the seam allowance open quite firmly. Now rip out the long stitches, turn the quilt and you will find you have an obvious straight crease line to follow when hand stitching.

Measuring Borders
Even if measurements are given for border strips, it is always worth double-checking against your own pieced top. Measure through the middle of the quilt, as the edges can become stretched.

Attaching Borders
Once you have determined the size of the top, bottom and side borders, fit the pieced top to these measurements rather than the other way round. Mark the centre and quarter points of the borders and of the quilt sides and match up. You may need to ease the sides of the quilt to fit the borders, but this will help to produce a flat, square quilt rather than one with wavy borders.

Storage
Store quilts in an old pillowcase or acid-free tissue paper rather than in a plastic bag, which doesn't allow fabrics to breathe and therefore encourages mould.

City Slicker

Designed by Nikki Foley

This bold, king-size bed quilt, made in beautiful warm colours, would look stunning in a modern apartment. Its large blocks grow quickly, making it a fast and satisfying project. For a smaller bed, you could either leave off the second border or make both borders narrower.

Finished size: 108 x 108 in/275 x 275 cm

MATERIALS
All fabrics used in the quilt top are 45 in/115 cm wide, 100% cotton.

Plain black squares and border 1: black, 3½ yds/3.2 m
Plain cream squares and border 2: cream, 2½ yds/ 2.5 m

Striped blocks: 20 in/50 cm each of five different tan/rust colours, and 20 in/50 cm each of five different light/dark red colours
Backing: 110 x 110 in/280 x 280 cm in colour of your choice
Wadding: 110 x 110 in/280 x 280 cm
Binding: 24 in/50 cm extra of one of the tan fabrics
Quilting thread

ALTERNATIVE COLOUR SCHEMES

1 Rich, warm colours for winter warmth; 2 Newly-weds would love the romantic touch of pastel green and peach; 3 Go wild with primary colours – red, yellow and blue; 4 A collection of blues is a great look for a bachelor pad.

CUTTING

NOTE When cutting fabric for any quilt, but especially a large one, it is a good idea to place the pieces into clear plastic bags (such as sandwich bags) as you cut them. Label them as you go along.

1 The black fabric is used both for the blocks and for the inner border – it is easier to cut the border strips first and then the squares. From the black fabric, cut ten strips across the width of the fabric, 5 in/12.75 cm deep. Put these to one side and label them "Border 1".

2 From the remaining black fabric, cut five strips across the width of the fabric, 13½ in/34.25 cm deep. Cut each strip into three 13½ x 13½ in/34.25 x 34.25 cm squares. You will need 13 black squares.

3 The cream fabric is used both for the blocks and for the outer border, so again cut the border first. From the cream fabric, cut ten strips across the width of the fabric, 3 in/7.5 cm deep. Put these to one side and label them "Border 2".

4 From the remaining cream fabric, cut four strips across the width of the fabric, 13½ in/34.25 cm deep. Cut each strip into three 13½ x 13½ in/34.25 x 34.25 cm squares. You will need 12 cream squares.

5 From each of the five tan/rust fabrics, cut seven strips across the width of the fabric, 2½ in/6.5 cm deep (total of 35 tan/rust strips).

6 From each of the five light/dark red fabrics, cut seven strips across the width of the fabric, 2½ in/6.5 cm deep (a total of 35 light/ dark red strips).

7 From the extra tan fabric, cut ten strips across the width of the fabric, 2 in/5 cm deep, for the binding.

STITCHING

1 Choose two different-coloured strips from the tan/rust strips and place them right sides together. Taking a ¼ in/0.75 cm seam allowance, stitch them together along one long edge. Using a different colour

of tan or rust for each strip, add another three strips in the same way, until you have stitched five strips together (diagram 1). Press all the seams downwards.

diagram 1

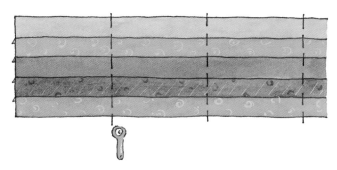

2 Trim ¼ in/0.5 cm off the top and bottom of the strip so that it measures 10 in/25.5 cm wide. Now treat the five stitched strips as one piece of fabric and cross-cut four 10 x 10 in/25.5 x 25.5 cm squares from the piece.

3 Repeat step 1 with the remaining tan/rust fabric strips, ensuring that you stitch them in the same order as the first five strips, until you have seven striped pieces in total. Then cross-cut each striped piece into four 10 x 10 in/25.5 x 25.5 cm squares, as in step 2 (you will need a total of 26 tan/rust striped squares).

4 Repeat steps 1-3, this time using the light/dark red strips (you will need a total of 26 light and dark red striped squares).

5 Place the tan/rust striped squares into two piles, with 13 squares in each pile. Taking one square at a time from pile 1, cut diagonally from A to D (diagram 2). Taking one square at a time from pile 2, cut diagonally from B to C. Once you have cut each square, keep the two halves together.

diagram 2

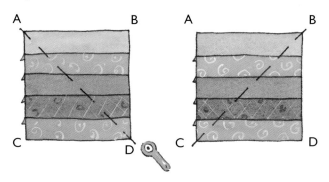

6 Take a matching pair of tan/rust striped triangles from pile 1. With right sides together, place the long diagonal side of one triangle to the top of a black 13½ x 13½ in/34.25 x 34.25 cm square. (The corners of the triangle should extend slightly beyond each corner of the square.) Taking a ¼ in/0.75 cm seam allowance, pin and stitch the triangle to the square. Then pin and stitch the long diagonal side of the second triangle to the bottom of the black square (diagram 3). Press the seams away from the centre square.

diagram 3

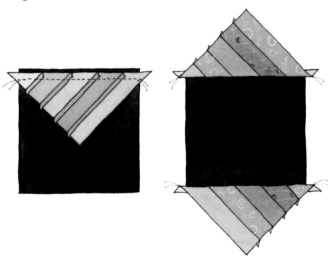

7 Now take a matching pair of tan/rust striped triangles from pile 2 and, taking the usual seam allowance, stitch one triangle on to each side of the black square (diagram 4). Continue stitching the tan/rust triangles on to the black squares until you have a total of 13 blocks.

diagram 4

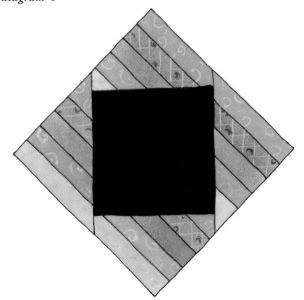

8 Repeat steps 5-7, using the light/dark red striped squares and the cream 13½ x 13½ in/34.25 x 34.25 cm squares until you have a total of 12 blocks.

9 Following the quilt plan on page 20 and taking a ¼ in/0.75 cm seam allowance, pin and stitch five blocks together to make row 1, being careful to have the strips going in alternating directions. Continue stitching rows of five blocks together until you have a total of five rows. Press all the seams open. Taking the usual seam allowance, pin and stitch the rows together. Again, press all the seams open.

ADDING THE BORDERS

1 As this is a big quilt, you will need to join two-and-a-half border strips together for each side. Start with the black Border 1. Measure the pieced top through the centre from side to side, then trim two of the joined black border strips to this measurement. Taking a ¼ in/0.75 cm seam allowance, pin and stitch to the top and bottom of the quilt.

2 Measure the pieced top through the centre from top to bottom, then trim two of the joined black border strips to this measurement. Taking the usual seam allowance, pin and stitch to each side.

3 Repeat steps 1 and 2 for the cream border, starting with the top and bottom, then the sides.

FINISHING

1 Spread the backing right side down on a flat surface, then smooth out the wadding and the patch-work top, right side up, on the top. Fasten together with safety pins or baste in a grid.

2 Quilt diagonally along the edge of the black and cream squares. Quilt a wavy or decorative stitch on to the borders.

3 Trim off any excess wadding and backing so they are even with the quilt top. Join the binding strips with diagonal seams to make a continuous length to fit all around the quilt and use to bind the edges with a double-fold binding, mitred at the corners.

Daisies and Snowballs

Designed by Gwen Jones

This queen-size bed quilt uses squares and half-square triangles to make up the rotating star block and the beautifully easy snowball block finished with fused appliqué. I used fabrics from one designer range, complemented with a subtle neutral to create a soft colour scheme. The advantage of using one range of fabrics is that it invariably incorporates a large print for borders and corresponding smaller prints and plains for the details. This, of course, speeds up the process of choosing suitable fabrics.

Finished size: 94 x 106 in/235 x 265 cm

MATERIALS
All fabrics used in the quilt top are 45 in/115 cm wide, 100% cotton.

Snowballs, triangles and corner squares: cream, 3½ yds/3.2 m
Snowballs, triangles and squares: pink fabrics, 3⅞ yds/ 3.5 m in total
Triangles: green fabrics, 32 in/80 cm in total

Border fabric 1 (pink floral): 1¼ yds/1.2 m
Border fabric 2 (green floral): 1⅞ yds/1.7 m
Daisies: scraps from above fabrics
Binding: 1 yd/90 cm green check
Fusible webbing: 18 in/50 cm
Backing fabric: 3 yds/2.75 m, 108 in/275 cm wide in colour of your choice
Wadding: 98 x 110 in/249 x 279 cm
Medium lead pencil
Invisible machine thread (optional)

ALTERNATIVE COLOUR SCHEMES

1 Peaches and cream combine to produce crisp, clean outlines; 2 Soft flannels in rust, tan and green and a mixture of florals and checks produce a warm quilt for winter; 3 Blue and off-white florals create a lovely country feel; 4 Experiment with rotating the stripes in this green and cream version.

1

2

3

4

CUTTING

1   From the cream fabric, cut the following:
20 squares, $12\frac{1}{2}$ in/31.5 cm;
44 squares, $4\frac{7}{8}$ in/12.5 cm;
4 squares, $5\frac{1}{2}$ in/14 cm;
4 squares, $6\frac{1}{2}$ in/16.5 cm.

2   From the green fabrics, cut 44 squares, $4\frac{7}{8}$ in/12.5 cm.

3   From the pink fabrics, cut the following:
80 squares, $4\frac{1}{2}$ in/11.5 cm (for snowball triangles);
110 squares, $4\frac{1}{2}$ in/11.5 cm.

4   From border fabric 1, cut eight strips across the width of the fabric, $5\frac{1}{2}$ in/14 cm deep.

5   From border fabric 2, cut eight strips across the width of the fabric, $6\frac{1}{2}$ in/16.5 cm deep.

6   From the binding fabric, cut ten strips across the width of the fabric, $2\frac{1}{2}$ in/6.5 cm deep.

STITCHING

1   Draw a light pencil line diagonally across the wrong side of each of the cream $4\frac{7}{8}$ in/12.5 cm squares. With right sides together, place one of these cream squares on top of one green $4\frac{7}{8}$ in/12.5 cm square. Stitch a $\frac{1}{4}$ in/0.75 cm seam on either side of the marked pencil line (diagram 1). Repeat for the remaining 43 squares.

diagram 1

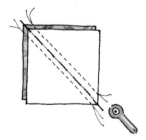

2   Press the seams flat to set them, then cut the squares apart along the pencil line to form two half-square triangle units. Press the units open, with the seam allowance pressed towards the darker fabric.

3   Using four triangle units and five pink $4\frac{1}{2}$ in/ 11.5 cm squares, lay out a block as shown in diagram 2. Taking a $\frac{1}{4}$ in/0.75 cm seam allowance and matching seams, stitch the block together as indicated. Repeat 21 times to make a total of 22 rotating blocks.

diagram 2

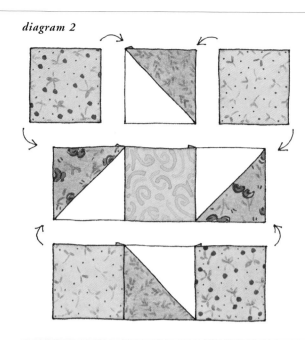

NOTE   The half-square triangle units rotate around the block. Be consistent and rotate them all the same way for each block.

4   Draw a light pencil line diagonally across the wrong side of each of the remaining 80 pink $4\frac{1}{2}$ in/11.5 cm squares.

5   With right sides together, place one pink square in each corner of a cream $12\frac{1}{2}$ in/31.5 cm square, so that the diagonal line is opposite the point of the square. Stitch along the pencil lines. Press the seams to set them and trim the seams to $\frac{1}{4}$ in/0.75 cm (diagram 3). Press the unit open to form one snowball block. Repeat 19 times to make a total of 20 snowball blocks.

diagram 3

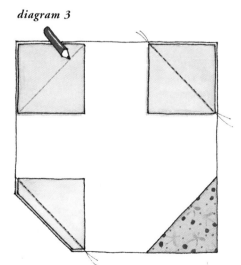

TEMPLATES
Actual size

Daisy Centre

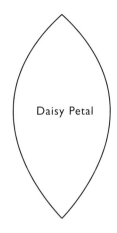

Daisy Petal

6 Trace the daisy petal template 120 times and the daisy centre template 20 times on to the paper side of the fusible webbing. Cut out, leaving a small margin around the tracings.

7 Using fabric left over from the construction of the blocks (I used all the pink fabrics for the petals and the green fabrics for the centres), fuse the webbing to the wrong side of fabric, following the manufacturer's instructions. Cut out along the traced lines.

8 Arrange a selection of six petals, fusible side down, in a circle in the centre of each snowball block. Press into position, following the manufacturer's instructions. Place one daisy centre in the middle, fusible side down, and press into position (diagram 4).

diagram 4

9 Thread your sewing machine with invisible thread in the top and a thread to match your fabric in the bobbin. Using a small zig-zag stitch, machine stitch around the appliqué pieces.

10 Following the quilt plan on page 26, lay out the blocks in seven rows of six blocks. Taking a $^1/_4$ in/ 0.75 cm seam allowance and matching the seams, pin and stitch the blocks together in rows. Press the seams to the left or right on alternate rows, so that the seams will butt together neatly in step 11.

11 Taking the usual seam allowance and matching the seams, pin and stitch the seven rows together. Press the seams downwards.

ADDING BORDER 1
Exact lengths are given for both borders but check these against your quilt first and make any adjustments necessary before cutting.
1 From the eight $5^1/_2$ in/14 cm wide strips, piece together strips to form two borders $72^1/_2$ in/181.5 cm in length and two borders $84^1/_2$ in/211.5 cm in length. Join a cream $5^1/_2$ in/14 cm square to either end of the two shorter borders. Taking the usual seam allowance, pin and stitch the two longer borders to the sides of the quilt. Press the seams towards the outer edge.

2 Pin and stitch the two borders with the cream squares to the top and bottom of the quilt, matching seams carefully. Press the seams as before.

ADDING BORDER 2
1 From the eight $6^1/_2$ in/16.5 cm wide strips, piece together strips to form two borders $82^1/_2$ in/206.5 cm in length and two borders $94^1/_2$ in/236.5 cm in length. Join a cream $6^1/_2$ in/16.5 cm square to either end of the two shorter borders. Taking the usual seam allowance, pin and stitch the two longer borders to the sides of the quilt. Press the seams towards the outer edge.

2 Pin and stitch the two borders with the cream squares to the top and bottom of the quilt, matching seams carefully. Press the seams as before.

FINISHING
1 Spread the backing right side down on a flat surface, then smooth out the wadding and the patchwork top, right side up, on top. Fasten together with safety pins or baste in a grid.

2 Using a decorative machine stitch, quilt "in the ditch" around the blocks. Then work free machine quilting around the daisies and rotating triangles.

3 Trim off any excess wadding and backing, so they are even with the quilt top. Join the binding strips with diagonal seams to make a continuous length to fit all around the quilt and use to bind the edges with a double-fold binding, mitred at the corners.

Irish Romance

Designed by Jane Coombes

Several fabrics blend together in this romantic-looking, king-size quilt. The central area is made from both quarter-square and half-square triangles, while the remainder consists of squares of varying sizes. The blocks featuring the smallest of these squares are based on the traditional "Irish Chain" block, which is why the quilt came to be named "Irish Romance". It could be made smaller by omitting the outer, pieced border.

Finished size: 108 x 108 in/256.5 x 256.5 cm

MATERIALS
All fabrics used in this quilt top are 45 in/115 cm
wide, 100% cotton.

Blocks: (The fabrics marked * include a quantity for
the borders)
3 yds/2.75 m royal blue*
2 yds/1.75 m royal blue and white floral*
3¹/₂ yds/3.25 m medium blue and white swirl*

1¹/₂ yds/1.25 m light blue and white
2 yds/1.75 m white
Backing: 9¹/₂ yds/8.5 m in colour of your choice
Wadding: 120 x 120 in/350 x 350 cm
Binding: royal blue, 28 in/70 cm
Sharp pencil
100% cotton thread
Invisible thread
Rayon machine embroidery thread

ALTERNATIVE COLOUR SCHEMES

The original design is based on four shades of one colour with a light shade of a contrasting colour. Two similar arrangements are shown in samples 1 and 2. Samples 3 and 4 use fabrics with more strongly contrasting colours, giving less of a blended effect. 1 Shades of pink and white are restful; 2 Apricot and cream make a light, subtle quilt; 3 Large and small prints matched with solid colours are lively; 4 Black, gold and beige have a more masculine appeal.

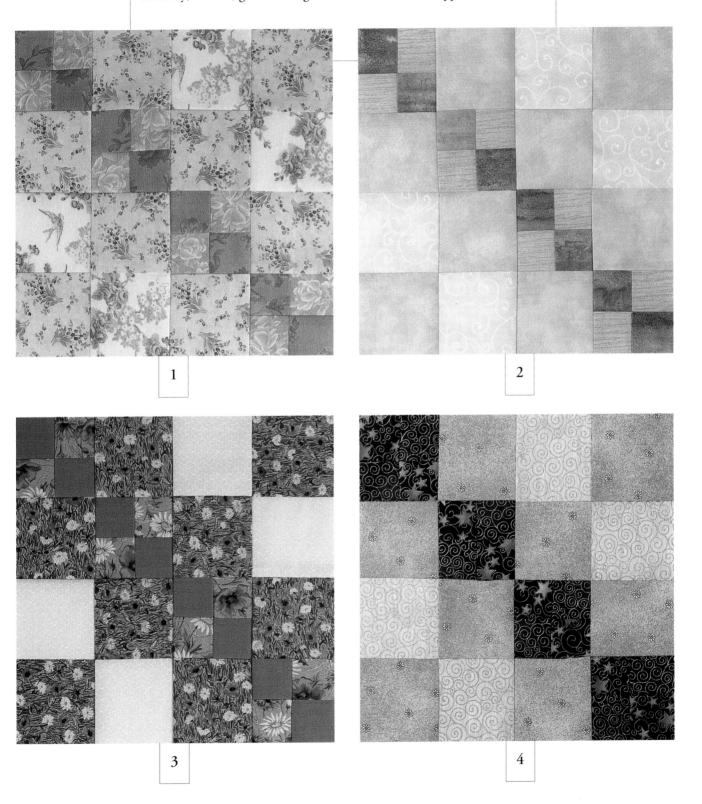

1

2

3

4

CUTTING

Cut all the following strips across the width of the fabric.

1 From the royal blue fabric cut:
a) four 8½ in/20.5 cm wide strips. Cross-cut into sixteen 8½ in/20.5 cm squares.
b) ten 2½ in/6.25 cm wide strips.
c) one 8⅞ in/22 cm wide strip. Cross-cut into four 8⅞ in/22 cm squares.
d) one 9¼ in/23 cm wide strip. Cross-cut into two 9¼ in/23 cm squares.
e) ten 2½ in/6.25cm wide strips. These are for border 1.

2 From the royal blue and white floral fabric cut:
a) one 8½ in/20.5 cm wide strip. Cross-cut into four 8½ in/20.5 cm squares.
b) ten 2½ in/6.25 cm wide strips.
c) one 8⅞ in/22 cm wide strip. Cross-cut into four 8⅞ in/22 cm squares.
d) one 9¼ in/23 cm wide strip. Cross-cut into two 9¼ in/23 cm squares.
e) three 4½ in/11 cm wide strips. Cross-cut into twenty-four 4½ in/11 cm squares. These are for border 2.

3 From the medium blue and white swirl fabric cut:
a) eighteen 4½ in/11 cm wide strips. Cross-cut nine of these strips into eighty 4½ in/11 cm squares.
b) six 4½ in/11 cm wide strips. Cross-cut into eight 4½ in/11 cm x 16½ in/39.5 cm rectangles and sixteen 4½ in/11 cm x 12½ in/30 cm rectangles. These are for border 2.

4 From the light blue and white fabric cut:
a) four 8½ in/20.5 cm wide strips. Cross-cut into twenty 8½ in/20.5 cm squares.
b) one 9¼ in/23 cm wide strip. Cross-cut into four 9¼ in/23 cm squares.

5 From the white fabric cut:
a) two 8½ in/20.5 cm wide strips. Cross-cut into eight 8½ in/20.5 cm squares.
b) nine 4½ in/11 cm wide strips.

6 Cut the backing across the width of the fabric into three equal lengths.

7 For the binding, cut eleven 2¼ in/5.75 cm wide strips.

STITCHING

NOTE ¼ in/0.75 cm seam allowances are used throughout.

1 Using a sharp pencil, draw a diagonal line on the wrong side of one light blue and white 9¼ in/23 cm square. Place, right sides together, against a royal blue square of the same size. Pin, then stitch ¼ in/0.75 cm either side of the drawn line. Carefully cut apart on the drawn line and press the seams towards the royal blue fabric (diagram 1).

diagram 1

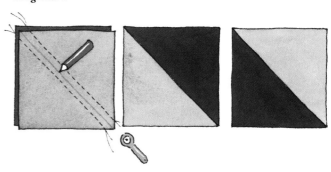

NOTE Press the seam as stitched before cutting apart to embed the stitches and to avoid stretching.

2 Draw a diagonal line on the wrong side of two royal blue 8⅞ in/22 cm squares. Place, right sides together, against the squares constructed in step 1 so that the drawn line and the stitching line cross each other in opposite directions, forming an X shape. Pin, then stitch either side of the drawn line and cut apart as before. Press the seams towards the half-square triangles (diagram 2). This makes four blocks.

diagram 2

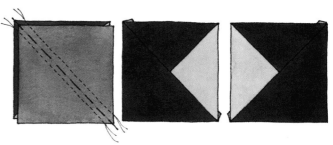

3 Draw a diagonal line on the wrong side of one light blue and white 9¼ in/23 cm square. Using a royal blue and white floral square of the same size, continue as in step 1, pressing the seams towards the darker fabric. Follow step 2 to make four more blocks.

4 Using one royal blue and white floral and one light blue and white 9¼ in/23 cm square together with two royal blue and white floral 8⅞ in/22 cm squares, make four more blocks as before.

5 Using one royal blue and one light blue and white 9¼ in/23 cm square together with two royal blue and white floral 8⅞ in/22 cm squares, make four more blocks.

6 Take 16 royal blue and 16 light blue and white 8½ in/20.5 cm squares and join them into two-colour pairs. Press the seam allowances towards the darker fabric. Arrange the pairs so that the same colour squares are diagonally opposite each other and stitch together (diagram 3). Press seam allowances to one side. Make eight large four-patch blocks in this way.

diagram 3

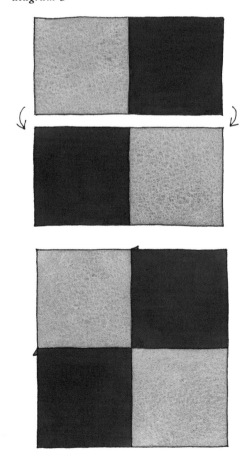

NOTE If possible, when joining the pairs of units, place the top seams facing the needle of the sewing machine and the bottom seams facing away from the needle in order to achieve perfect matching.

7 Using four royal blue and white floral, four light blue and white, and eight white 8½ in/20.5 cm squares, make the remaining large four-patch blocks as in step 6.

8 With right sides together, stitch nine medium blue and white swirl and nine white 4½ in/11 cm wide strips together in two-colour pairs along their long edges. Press the seam allowances towards the darker fabric. Cross-cut into 80 x 4½ in/11 cm units (diagram 4). Arrange these units as in step 6 to make 40 medium-size four-patch blocks.

diagram 4

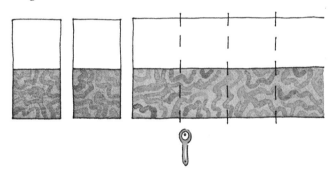

9 Using ten royal blue and ten royal blue and white floral 2½ in/6.25 cm wide strips, work as in step 8, cross-cutting them into 160 x 2½ in/6.25 cm units and joining them to make 80 small four-patch blocks.

10 Using the 80 medium blue and white swirl 4½ in/11 cm squares and the 80 small four-patch blocks made in step 9, construct 40 medium-size four-patch blocks (diagram 5). Press the seams towards the small four-patch blocks when joining the units into pairs, then to one side when completing the blocks.

diagram 5

Following diagram 6, join the blocks from step 8 to those from step 10. Press the seams towards the blocks from step 8 when joining the units into pairs, then to one side when completing the blocks. This makes a total of 20 blocks.

diagram 6

JOINING THE BLOCKS

1 Lay out the blocks following the quilt plan on page 32. Using a ¼ in/0.75 cm seam allowance, join the sixteen blocks for the central section into rows and press the seams to one side.

NOTE Press the seam allowances of row 1 to the left, row 2 to the right, row 3 to the left, and so on. This will help you match the seams accurately when you join the rows.

2 Join the rows to complete the central section. Press the seams towards the bottom of the quilt.

3 Join the four-patch blocks from steps 6 and 7 and stitch these to the central section as before.

4 Join the blocks from step 11 in the same way.

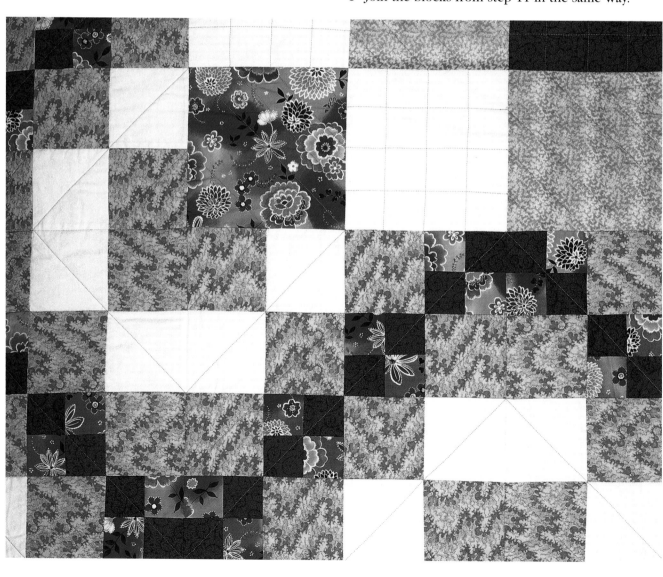

ADDING THE BORDERS

1 Join the royal blue 2½ in/6.25 cm wide strips for border 1 together across the short ends to make a long strip. This is best done with diagonal seams and sufficient fabric has been allowed for this method.

2 Measure the pieced top through the centre from top to bottom, then cut two strips to this measurement from the strip joined in step 1.

3 Fold each border strip in half lengthwise and pin-mark the centre point. Pin-mark the centre of the quilt sides in same way.

4 Repeat step 3 as often as necessary so that both border strips and quilt side edges are pin-marked at regular intervals. With right sides together and matching the pin-markers, pin both layers together, easing gently if necessary. Stitch, taking a ¼ in/0.75 cm seam allowance. Press the seams towards the border.

5 Measure the pieced top through the centre from side to side, then cut two strips to this measurement. Pin and stitch to the top and bottom edges of quilt, following steps 3 and 4 above.

6 Join the medium blue and white swirl 4½ in/ 11 cm wide strips and the royal blue and white floral 4½ in/11 cm squares together as shown in diagram 7 to make four border strips for border 2.

diagram 7

7 Taking care to match the border 2 squares to the corresponding squares adjacent to the inside edge of border 1, attach two of these strips to the quilt sides, following steps 3-4. Press the seams towards border 1.

8 Join one royal blue and white floral 4½ in/11 cm square to each end of the remaining two border strips. Attach these strips to the top and bottom edges of the quilt as before.

FINISHING

1 Cut the selvages from the backing fabric and, taking a ½ in/1.5 cm seam allowance, stitch the three lengths of fabric together along the trimmed edges. Press the seams open.

2 Spread the backing right side down on a flat surface, then smooth out the wadding and the patch-work top, right side up, on top. Fasten together with safety pins or baste in a grid.

3 Machine quilt in-the-ditch round the blocks, using invisible thread on the spool and 100% cotton thread in a colour to match the backing fabric on the bobbin. Add further lines of straight machine quilting (diagram 8), using a rayon machine embroidery thread on the spool and the same thread as before on the bobbin.

diagram 8

NOTE Use a walking/even-feed foot on your sewing machine when stitching through three or more layers to prevent tucks on the underneath fabrics.

4 Trim off the excess wadding and backing in line with the quilt top. Join the binding strips with diagonal seams to make a continuous length to fit all round the quilt and use to bind the edges with a double-fold binding, mitred at the corners.

Prairie Plaids

Designed by Katharine Guerrier

Plaids and striped fabrics in a wide variety of colours and scales are used to make this queen-size quilt, giving it the appeal of a traditional scrap quilt. Simple blocks, each made from eight triangles, are set on point and arranged in a contrasting formation to create a checkerboard effect. The size can be easily adjusted by varying the number of blocks. The quilting was done on a longarm quilting machine by Rosemary Archer.

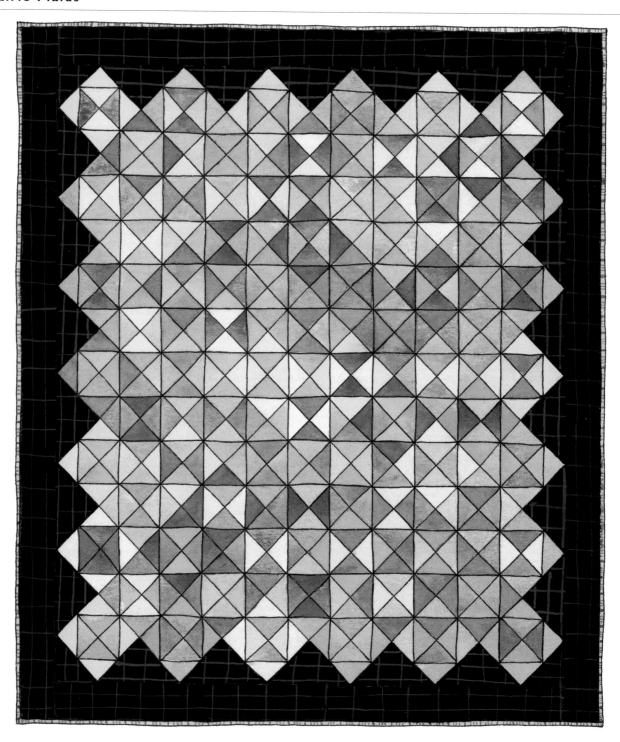

Finished size: 99 x 113½ in/251 x 288 cm

MATERIALS

All fabrics used in the quilt top are 45 in/115 cm wide, 100 % cotton.

Blocks: A total of 7 yds/6.5 m of scrap pieces in plaids and stripes, each measuring at least 6 in/ 15.25 cm square

Corner triangles, side triangles and borders: 3½ yds/ 3.25 m brown plaid

Binding: 30 in/75 cm yellow stripe

Backing: 106 x 120 in/270 x 305 cm in colour of your choice

Wadding: 2 oz or low loft, 106 x 120 in/270 x 305 cm

Machine quilting thread

ALTERNATIVE COLOUR SCHEMES

1 Blue fabrics create a tranquil atmosphere in any décor; 2 Printed fabrics in warm tones and a variety of scales provide visual texture; 3 Printed flannels would make a soft, warm bedcover; 4 Brightly coloured prints featuring dots and stars create a mood of energy and movement.

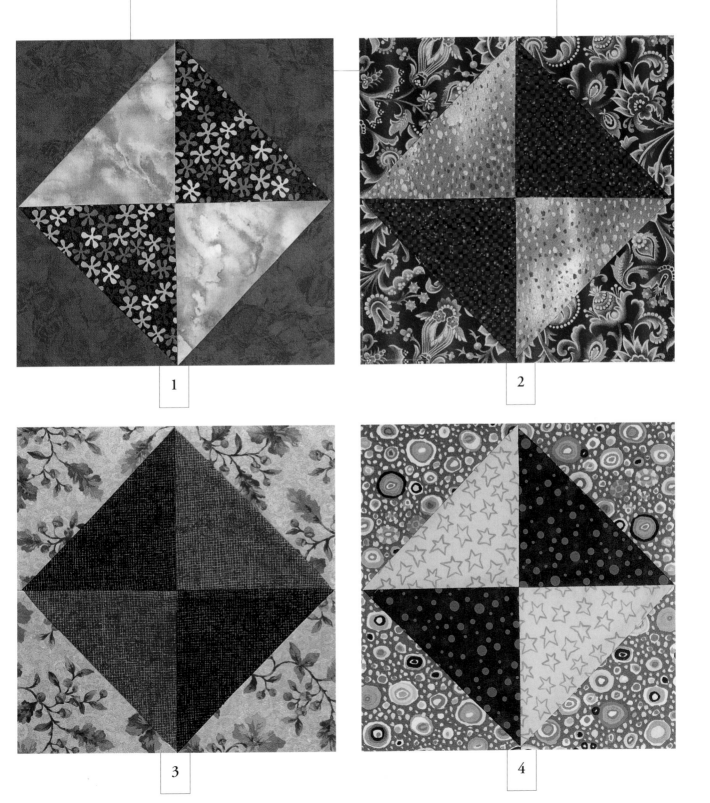

CUTTING

1 From the brown plaid fabric, cut two strips, 6½ x 90 in/16.5 x 229 cm, and two strips, 6½ x 118 in/16.5 x 299.5 cm, for the borders.

2 From the brown plaid fabric, cut five 15½ in/ 39.5 cm squares and cross-cut each one into four triangles by cutting across both diagonals. Use one of the resulting triangles as a template to cut two more triangles (total of 22 side triangles).

3 From the brown plaid fabric, cut two 8 in/20.5 cm squares and cross-cut each one into two triangles by cutting across one diagonal (total of four corner triangles).

4 From the 30 in/75 cm piece of yellow stripe fabric, cut nine strips across the width of the fabric, 2¾ in/7 cm deep, for the binding.

5 Cut patches for the blocks from the plaids and striped fabrics as you work.

STITCHING

1 For one block, cut four 6 in/15.25 cm squares in three different fabrics: two of fabric A, and one each of fabrics B and C. Try to contrast the three fabrics by choosing different colours, tonal values or scales in the patterns.

2 Place one A/B fabric pair right sides together and one A/C fabric pair right sides together. Draw one diagonal line from corner to corner and stitch ¼ in/0.75 cm on both sides of the line (diagram 1).

diagram 1

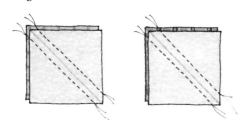

3 Cut across the diagonal to make two half-square triangle units in each combination. Press the seam allowance towards the darker fabric. Trim off the small "ears" of fabric that extend beyond the square.

4 Arrange the units as shown in diagram 2a. Taking a ¼ in/0.75 cm seam allowance, pin and stitch the block together in the order indicated (diagram 2b). Press the seams open.

diagram 2a

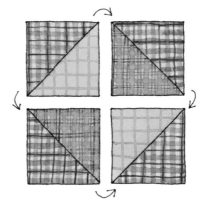

diagram 2b

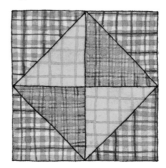

5 Using the remaining plaids and striped fabrics, repeat steps 1-4 to make a total of 72 blocks.

6 Following the quilt plan on page 40 lay out the blocks in diagonal rows, changing the positioning of the blocks until you are happy with the arrangement.

7 Taking the usual seam allowance, pin and stitch the blocks in diagonal rows, adding the side and corner triangles as you work (diagram 3). Press the seams towards the blocks, pressing towards opposite sides on alternate rows, so that when you join the rows, the seams will butt together well.

diagram 3

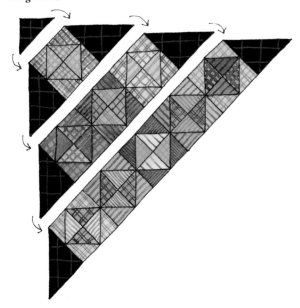

8 Taking the usual seam allowance, pin and stitch the rows together, matching the seams.

ADDING THE BORDERS

1 Measure the pieced top through the centre from side to side, then trim the two shorter border strips to this measurement. Taking a ¼ in/0.75 cm seam allowance, pin and stitch to the top and bottom of the quilt.

2 Measure the pieced top through the centre from top to bottom, then trim the two remaining border strips to this measurement. Taking the usual seam allowance, pin and stitch to the sides.

FINISHING

1 Spread the backing right side down on a flat surface, then smooth out the wadding and the patchwork top, right side up, on top. Fasten together with safety pins or baste in a grid.

2 Using machine quilting thread, quilt over the surface of the quilt with "free motion" quilting.

3 Join the binding strips with straight seams to make four lengths to bind the top, bottom and sides of the quilt. Fold the strips in half lengthways to create a double binding.

4 Trim off any excess wadding and backing so they are even with the quilt top. Place the longer binding strips, raw edges to raw edges, along the sides of the quilt. Pin in place and stitch, taking a ¼ in/0.75 cm seam allowance. Turn the binding over to the back of the quilt. Slip-stitch in place using a matching thread.

5 Turn under the raw edges at each end of the shorter binding strips. Stitch to the top and bottom of the quilt as in step 4.

Sister's Choice

Designed by Katharine Guerrier

Many of the traditional American blocks have more than one name. In addition to "Sister's Choice", this one is also known as "Farmer's Daughter". Whatever the name, the pieced five-patch blocks, in a selection of contemporary prints and set on point with alternate cream setting squares, will make an elegant double-bed quilt for a summer bedroom. The quilting was done on a longarm quilting machine by Rosemary Archer.

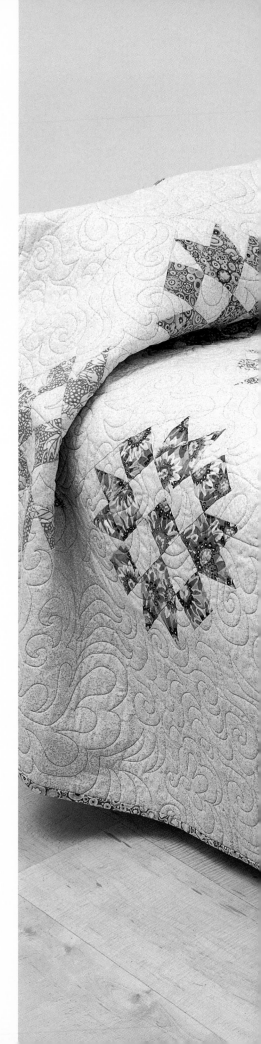

Finished size: 93 x 109 in/233 x 272 cm

MATERIALS

All fabrics used in the quilt top are 45 in/115 cm wide, 100 % cotton.

Blocks, border, side triangles and corner triangles:
7½ yds/7 m of cream all-over print
Blocks: 24 in/50 cm each of five harmonizing patterned prints

Marking pencil
Backing: 101 x 117 in/257 x 298 cm in colour of your choice
Wadding: 2 oz or low loft, 101 x 117 in/ 257 x 298 cm
Binding: 32 in/75 cm extra of one of the five harmonizing patterned prints
Machine quilting thread

ALTERNATIVE COLOUR SCHEMES

1 Hand-dyed fabrics in four colours have been used in this sample; 2 Dot prints in strong, bright colours create an exuberant mood; 3 The subtle contrast in this block is created by a change of scale in the prints; 4 Blue and cream would give an air of tranquillity to a cool, summer bedroom.

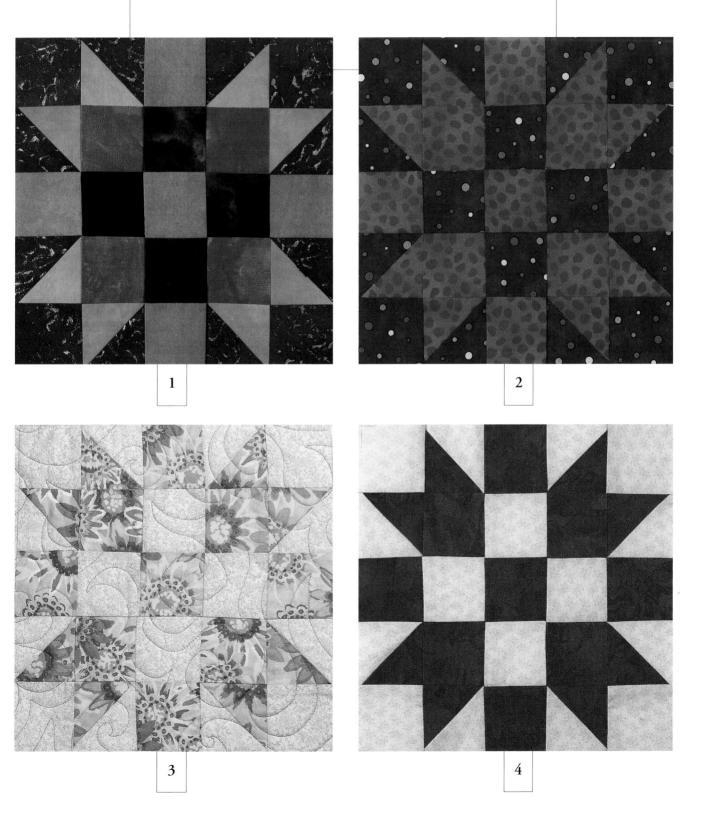

1

2

3

4

CUTTING

Cut the cream fabric for the border, side triangles and corner triangles at this stage. Cut the remaining fabrics as you work.

1 From the cream fabric, cut two strips, 7 x 82 in/ 18 x 209 cm, and two strips, 7 x 110 in/18 x 282 cm, for the border.

2 From the cream fabric, cut twenty 11¼ in/ 28.5 cm squares for the alternate squares.

3 From the cream fabric, cut four 17¼ in/44 cm squares and cross-cut these into four triangles by cutting across both diagonals. Use one of these triangles as a template to cut two more triangles (total of 18 side triangles).

4 From the cream fabric, cut two 9 in/23 cm squares and cross-cut these into two triangles each by cutting across one diagonal (total of four corner triangles).

STITCHING

Steps 1 to 7 describe how to cut and stitch six blocks using one of the print fabrics.

1 From across the width of one of the print fabrics, cut two strips, 3⅛ in/8 cm deep, and three strips, 2¾ in/7 cm deep. Cut the same from the cream fabric. From these strips, cut one cream and one patterned strip, 2¾ x 41 in/7 x 104 cm. Place these two strips right sides together and, taking a ¼ in/0.75 cm seam allowance, stitch along one long side. Cross-cut into twelve 2¾ in/7 cm segments (diagram 1).

diagram 1

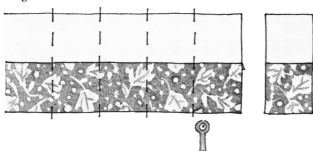

2 From the same print fabric, cut three strips, 2¾ x 18 in/7 x 46 cm. From the cream fabric, cut two strips, 2¾ x 18 in/7 x 46 cm. Stitch these together in the sequence: print/cream/print/cream/print. Cross-cut into six 2¾ in/7 cm segments (diagram 2).

diagram 2

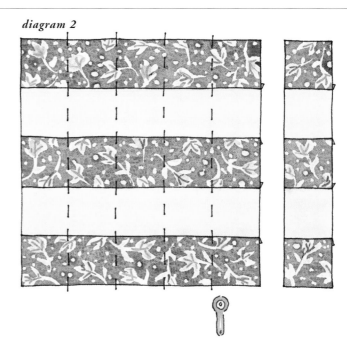

3 From the remaining cream fabric, cut twenty-four 2¾ in/7 cm squares. From the remaining print fabric, cut twenty-four 2¾ in/7 cm squares.

4 From the 3⅛ in/8 cm strips, cut six cream and six print strips, 14 in/35.5 cm long. With right sides together, pair up each cream strip with one of the print strips. On the wrong side of each cream strip, mark off four 3⅛ in/8 cm squares. Then draw a continuous zig-zag line from corner to corner of the marked squares along the length of the strip. Stitch along both sides of these lines, ¼ in/0.75cm away (diagram 3a).

diagram 3a   *diagram 3b*

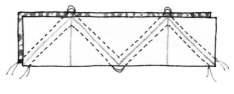

NOTE You can stitch in a continuous line, using a ¼ in/0.75 cm foot on your sewing machine. If you do not have this facility, mark the sewing line before stitching.

5 Cut along the marked vertical and diagonal lines. Press the seams of the resulting half-square triangle units towards the print side and trim off the small "ears" of fabric that extend beyond the square (total of 48 units) (diagram 3b).

6 Following diagram 4, pin and stitch two of the half-square triangle units, one print 2¾ in/7 cm square and one cream 2¾ in/7 cm square to make the corner sections for the blocks (total of 24 corner sections).

diagram 4

7 Lay out the first block in the sequence shown in diagram 5 as follows: four corner sections, two two-square segments (see step 1) and one five-square segment (see step 2). Taking a ¼ in/0.75 cm seam allowance, pin and stitch the block together as illustrated, keeping the orientation of the seams correct. Make five more blocks from the remaining units.

diagram 5

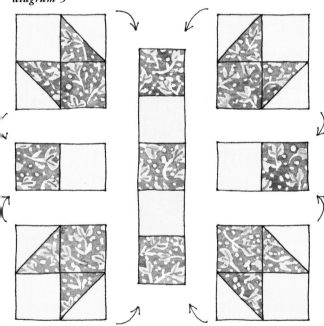

8 Repeat steps 1-7, using the remaining print fabrics combined with the cream fabric to make a total of 30 blocks.

9 Press the pieced blocks thoroughly. If necessary, trim the alternate setting squares, previously cut from the cream fabric, to fit the pieced blocks.

10 Following the quilt plan on page 46, lay out the blocks in diagonal rows, alternating the pieced and plain squares. Change the positioning of the pieced blocks until you are happy with the arrangement.

11 Pin and stitch the pieced blocks alternating with the cream squares into diagonal rows, adding the corner and side triangles as you work (diagram 6). Press the seams towards the cream squares. Then pin and stitch the rows together, matching the seams.

diagram 6

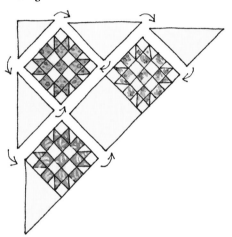

ADDING THE BORDERS

1 Measure the pieced top through the centre from side to side, then trim the two shorter cream border strips to this measurement. Taking a ¼ in/0.75 cm seam allowance, pin and stitch to the top and bottom of the quilt.

2 Measure the pieced top through the centre from top to bottom, then trim the remaining two cream border strips to this measurement. Taking the usual seam allowance, pin and stitch to each side of the quilt.

FINISHING

1 Spread the backing right side down on a flat surface, then smooth out the wadding and the patchwork top, right side up, on top. Fasten together with safety pins or baste in a grid.

2 Using machine quilting thread, quilt over the surface of the quilt with "free motion" quilting.

3 Trim off any excess wadding and backing level with the pieced top. Using the extra print fabric, cut ten strips, 2¾ in/7 cm wide. Join the binding strips with diagonal seams to make a continuous length to fit round the quilt and use to bind the edges with a double-fold binding, mitred at the corners.

Springtime Squares

Designed by Janet Goddard

This fresh, sunny, queen-size quilt has a spring-time theme. The fabrics used include florals, spots, stripes and small patterns in a yellow, green and orange colourway. The simple square-in-a-square repeating blocks showcase the delightful combination of fabrics.

Finished size: 90½ x 105½ in/226.5 x 263.5 cm

MATERIALS
All fabrics used in the quilt top are 45 in/115 cm wide, 100% cotton.

Yellow stripes: 2 yds/1.8 m
Yellow small floral print: 2 yds/1.8 m
Yellow large floral print: 2 yds/1.8 m
Orange print: 24 in/60 cm
Orange check: 24 in/60 cm

Green spot: 24 in/60 cm
Green print: 24 in/60 cm
Border: orange print fabric, 44 in/1.1 m
Binding: yellow floral fabric, 20 in/50 cm
Backing: 94 x 109 in/239 x 277 cm in colour of your choice
Wadding: 80/20 cotton/polyester, 94 x 109 in/ 239 x 277 cm
Invisible thread for quilting
Lemon cotton thread for quilting
Orange cotton thread for quilting

ALTERNATIVE COLOUR SCHEMES

1 Co-ordinating floral prints in two different sizes against a plain yellow background; 2 Bright red, yellow and blue prints with a yellow background; 3 Red, blue and beige small floral prints with a cream and beige background; 4 Autumn colours, browns and oranges with a touch of navy.

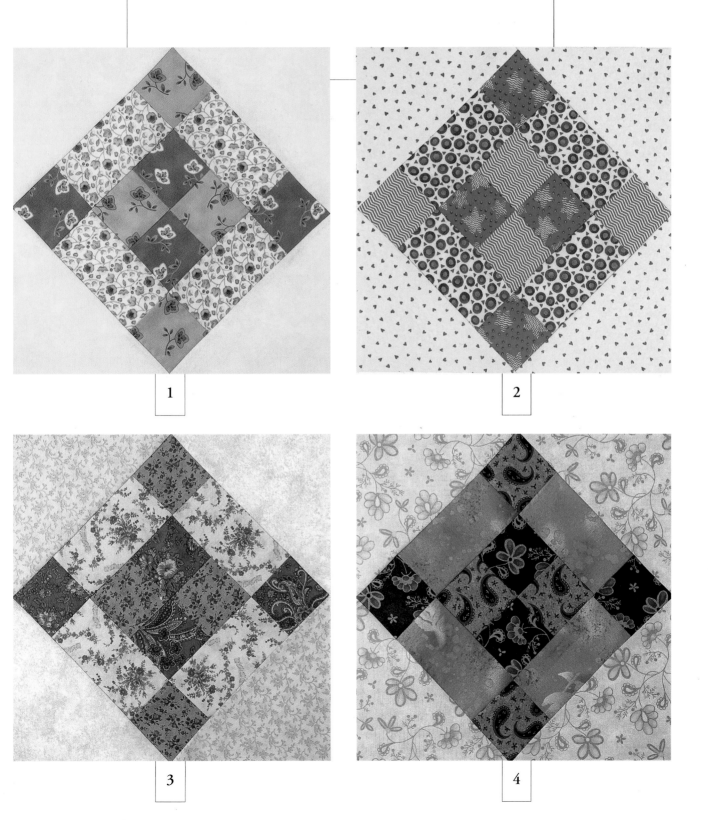

CUTTING

1 From the yellow striped fabric, cut 224 rectangles, 4¾ x 2⅝ in/12 x 6.5 cm.

2 From the yellow small floral print, cut 56 squares, 6⅞ in/17.5 cm, then cross-cut these on the diagonal once to yield 112 triangles.

3 From the yellow large floral print, cut 56 squares 6⅞ in/17.5 cm, then cross-cut these on the diagonal once to yield 112 triangles.

4 From each of the orange and green fabrics, cut 112 squares, 2⅝ in/6.5 cm.

5 From the border fabric, cut six strips across the width of the fabric, 3½ in/9 cm deep and four strips, 5 in/12.5 cm deep.

6 From the binding fabric, cut ten strips across the width of the fabric, 2 in/5 cm deep.

STITCHING THE BLOCKS

The blocks come in two different colour variations. Make 28 of each type of block.

1 Take two orange check squares and two green spot squares. Taking a ¼ in/0.75 cm seam allowance, stitch each orange square to a green one to make two matching pairs. Pin the matching pairs right sides together, reversing the colours and matching the centre seams. Stitch together into a four-patch unit (diagram 1).

diagram 1

2 Stitch a yellow striped rectangle to two opposite sides of the four-patch unit. Press the seams towards the rectangles.

3 Stitch an orange check square to one end of a yellow striped rectangle and a green spot square to the opposite end. Repeat with another yellow striped rectangle but reverse the position of the orange and green squares. Press the seams towards the rectangles.

4 Stitch the units made in step 3 to the four-patch unit made in step 2 (diagram 2).

diagram 2

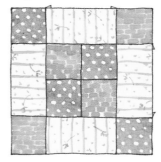

5 Take two yellow large floral print triangles and stitch them to opposite sides of the completed square unit. Press the seams towards the triangle.

NOTE Once you have stitched the triangles to the square, there should be ¼ in/0.75 cm triangle points protruding at each end for seam allowances.

6 Take two yellow small floral print triangles and stitch them to the remaining two sides of the square. Press the seams towards the triangles. Trim off any extended points. This completes Block 1 (diagram 3).

diagram 3

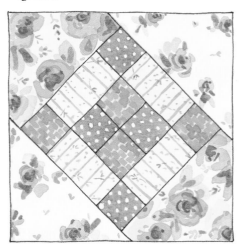

7   Repeat steps 1-6 to stitch 28 blocks in total, remembering to keep the fabrics in exactly the same positions.

8   Repeat steps 1-7 to stitch another 28 blocks (Block 2) but substitute the orange print squares for the orange check squares and the green print squares for the green spot squares (diagram 4).

diagram 4

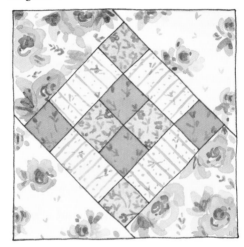

ASSEMBLING THE BLOCKS

1   Following the quilt plan on page 52, lay out the blocks in eight rows of seven blocks, alternating Block 1 with Block 2, and the large floral print triangles with the small floral print triangles. Alternate the blocks row by row, too.

2   Taking a ¼ in/0.75 cm seam allowance, pin and stitch the blocks together in horizontal rows. Press the seams in the first row to the right and the seams in the second row to the left. Press the seams alternately to the right or left for the remaining rows.

3   Taking the usual seam allowance and matching the seams, pin and stitch the rows together. Press the seams downwards.

ADDING THE BORDERS

1   Stitch the six 3 ½ in/9 cm border strips together into one long strip.

2   Stitch the four 5 in/12.5 cm border strips together into one long strip.

3   Measure the pieced top through the centre from side to side and cut two strips to this measurement from the 5 in/12.5 cm strips. Taking a ¼ in/0.75 cm seam allowance, pin and stitch to the top and bottom of the quilt. Press the seams towards the borders.

4   Measure the pieced top through the centre from top to bottom and cut two strips to this measurement from the 3½ in/9 cm strips. Taking the usual seam allowance, pin and stitch to the sides of the quilt. Press the seams towards the borders.

FINISHING

1   Spread the backing right side down on a flat surface, then smooth out the wadding and the patchwork top, right side up, on top. Fasten together with safety pins or baste in a grid.

2   Use the invisible thread to quilt in the ditch around each central four-patch unit.

3   Use the lemon thread to quilt ½ in/1.5 cm in from the seam line around each four-triangle floral print square and each two-triangle floral print unit (the two-triangle units are situated around the edge of the quilt).

4   Use the orange thread to quilt a random square-and-line pattern on the border (diagram 5).

diagram 5

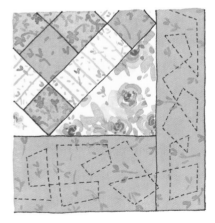

5   Trim off any excess wadding and backing, so they are even with the quilt top. Stitch the binding strips with diagonal seams to make a continuous length to fit all around the quilt and use to bind the edges with a double-fold binding, mitred at the corners.

Tangerine Sunburst

Designed by Janet Goddard

This bright, sunny, queen-size quilt evokes memories of hot summer days. The quilt features repeating Dresden plate blocks, which are stitched using a quick and easy method. The blocks are joined by thin sashing with yellow corner squares and the patchwork is finished with simple quilting.

Finished size: 90 x 111 in/227 x 280 cm

MATERIALS
All fabrics used in the quilt top are 45 in/115 cm wide, 100% cotton.

Background: cream print, 6¼ yds/5.5 m
Dresden plates: 40 in/1 m each of five fabrics – dark orange, orange check, yellow/orange spot, orange swirl and yellow/orange flower print
Sashing and Dresden plate centres: plain orange, 1⅔ yds/1.5 m

Small corner squares: yellow, 6 in/16 cm
Border: one of fabrics from Dresden plate blocks, 1⅔ yds/1.5 m
Backing: 94 x 115 in/237 x 290 cm in colour of your choice
Wadding: 94 x 115 in/237 x 290 cm
Binding: plain cream, 30 in/75 cm
Template plastic: 8 in/21 cm square
Neutral thread for piecing
Invisible thread for stitching folded edges
Fusible webbing: 20 in/50 cm
Cream cotton quilting thread

ALTERNATIVE COLOUR SCHEMES

1 Five different 1930s reproduction fabrics combine well to make a lovely soft colour scheme; 2 Five shades of blue against the calico background make a crisp, fresh design; 3 Just two pale green pastel prints produce a really restful design; 4 Perennially popular red and green Christmas prints make a fabulous quilt for a holiday visitor.

1

2

3

4

TEMPLATES
Actual size

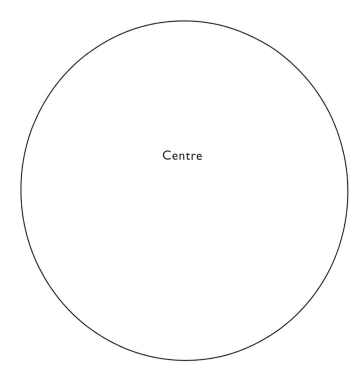

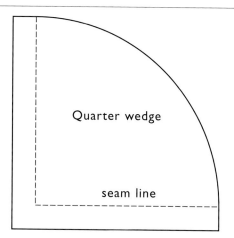

Small wedge

Quarter wedge

seam line

Centre

Wedge

CUTTING

1   From the cream print background fabric, cut 20 squares, 18½ x 18½ in/47 x 47 cm, and eight strips, 4½ x 18½ in/11.5 x 47 cm.

2. Using the template plastic, make a template of the large wedge and use it to mark and cut 80 wedges from each of the five Dresden plate fabrics.

3   Using the template plastic, make a template of the small wedge and use it to mark and cut four wedges from each of the five Dresden plate fabrics.

4   From the plain orange sashing fabric, cut 57 strips, 18½ x 1½ in/47 x 4 cm, and 10 strips, 4½ x 1½ in/ 11.5 x 4 cm.

5 From the yellow fabric, cut 40 squares, 1½ x 1½ in/ 4 x 4 cm.

6 From the border fabric, cut two strips, 2¾ x 77½ in/ 7 x 196 cm, and two strips, 6¾ x 111½ in/17 x 285.5 cm. You will need to stitch strips together to achieve the required lengths.

7 From the cream binding fabric, cut two strips, 2 x 91 in/5 x 228 cm, and two strips, 2 x 111 in/ 5 x 280 cm. You will need to stitch strips together to achieve the required lengths.

STITCHING THE DRESDEN PLATE BLOCKS

Each Dresden plate block is made up of five fabrics, each repeated four times, i.e. each block consists of 20 wedges. To make one block:

1 Lay out 20 large wedges in the order that you wish to stitch them together. I have alternated dark and light fabrics.

2 Take the first wedge and fold it with right sides together. Using the neutral thread, stitch a ¼ in/ 0.75 cm seam across the wide end of the wedge. At the inner edge, reverse the stitching a short way to secure the thread (diagram 1). Clip the inner corner.

diagram 1

3 Turn the wedge right side out and press the seam so that it is centred at the back of the wedge (diagram 2). Repeat steps 2 and 3 for the remaining wedges.

diagram 2

4 The wedges are stitched together in a repeated sequence. To begin, place two wedges right sides together and start stitching ¼ in/0.75 cm down from the outer end, reverse to the edge and then stitch forwards (diagram 3).

diagram 3

5 Stitch all 20 wedges together in the same way and press all the seams in the same direction.

6 Pin the completed Dresden plate centrally on to a cream print background square.

7 Using invisible thread and a straight stitch, stitch the Dresden plate in place ⅛ in/0.3 cm in from the outer folded edge (diagram 4).

diagram 4

8 Trace the centre circle template on to fusible webbing. Cut out and iron on to the reverse of the plain orange fabric. Cut out the fabric and bond to the centre of the Dresden plate. Using a zig-zag stitch, carefully stitch around the outer edge of the circle to secure in position.

9 Repeat steps 1-8 to make a total of 20 Dresden plate blocks.

ASSEMBLING THE BLOCKS

1 Following the quilt assembly diagram, lay out the Dresden plate blocks in five rows of four blocks.

2 Pin and stitch the blocks into rows with an 18½ x 1½ in/47 x 4 cm sashing strip between each block and one at each end. Press the seams towards the sashing.

3 To make the sashing between the rows, stitch four sashing strips together with a 1½ in/4 cm corner square linking each strip and one at each end. Press the seams towards the sashing strips. Make a total of eight lengths of pieced sashing in this way.

4 Pin and stitch all the rows together with four lengths of pieced sashing in between and two lengths at the top and bottom.

STITCHING THE TOP AND BOTTOM BORDERS

1 Stitch the 20 small wedges into four groups of five, using the same technique as for the main blocks. This will make four quarter Dresden plate shapes.

2 Take four of the 4½ x 18½ in/11.5 x 47 cm cream print background strips. Place a quarter Dresden plate on the right-hand side of two of the strips and on the left-hand side of the remaining two strips. Use the invisible thread and a straight stitch to stitch around the outer edge of the Dresden plates ⅛ in/0.3 cm in from the folded edge.

3 Trace the quarter circle template on to fusible webbing. Cut out and iron on to the reverse of the plain orange fabric for the centre. Cut out the fabric and bond to the centre of a quarter Dresden plate (diagram 5). Using a zig-zag stitch, carefully stitch around the outer edge of the circle. Repeat for the remaining quarter Dresden plates.

diagram 5

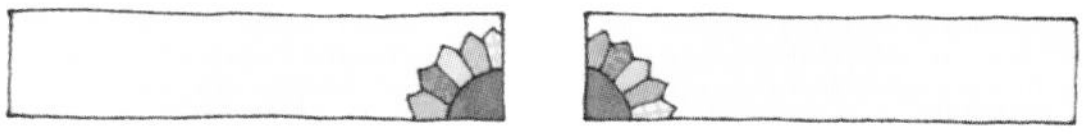

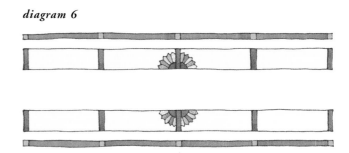

4 Lay out the top and bottom borders so that there are four 4½ x 18½ in/11.5 x 47 cm background strips in a row with the quarter Dresden plates forming a semicircle in the centre. Stitch the background strips together with a 4½ x 1½ in/11.5 x 4 cm sashing strip between each and one at each end (diagram 6).

diagram 6

5 Pin and stitch the borders to the top and bottom of the quilt.

6 Stitch the remaining two lengths of pieced sashing to the top and bottom of the quilt (see diagram 6).

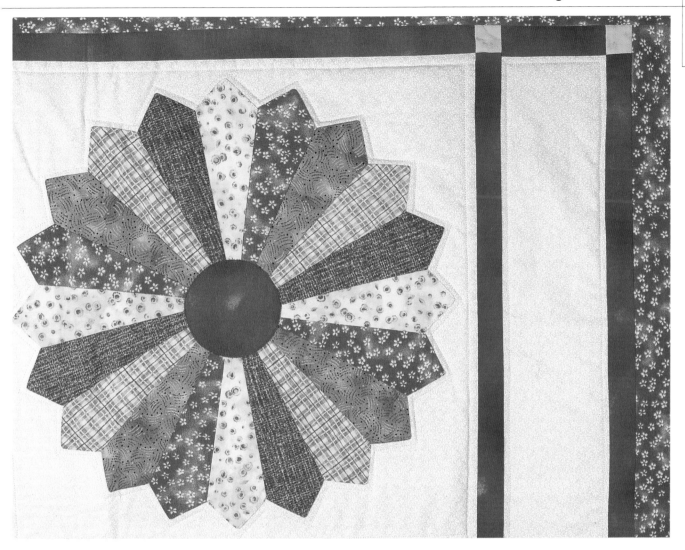

ADDING THE OUTER BORDERS

1 Measure the patchwork top through the centre from side to side. Adjust the length of the two 2³⁄₄ x 77¹⁄₂ in/7 x 196 cm border strips as necessary, then pin and stitch to the top and bottom.

2 Measure the patchwork top through the centre from top to bottom. Adjust the length of the two 6³⁄₄ x 111¹⁄₂ in/17 x 281.5 cm border strips as necessary, then pin and stitch to each side.

FINISHING

1 Spread the backing right side down on a flat surface, then smooth out the wadding and the patchwork top, right side up, on top. Fasten together with safety pins or baste in a grid.

2 Using the cream thread, quilt ¹⁄₂ in/1.5 cm in from the outer edge of each background square. Quilt ¹⁄₄ in/0.75 cm away from the folded edges of the Dresden plates.

3 Using the invisible thread, quilt around each Dresden plate centre.

4 Trim off any excess wadding and backing so they are even with the quilt top. With wrong sides facing, press each binding strip in half along the length of the strip.

5 Place the longer binding strips, raw edges to raw edges, along the sides of the quilt. Pin in place and stitch, taking a ¹⁄₄ in/0.75 cm seam allowance. Fold the edge of the binding under and turn the binding over to the back of the quilt. Slip stitch in place using a matching thread.

6 Turn under the raw edges at each end of the shorter binding strips. Stitch to the top and bottom of the quilt as in step 5.

Squares and Stars

Designed by Alison Wood

A variety of reproduction Thirties prints make up the scrappy sixteen-patch blocks, which are speedily put together using strip cutting and chain piecing methods. Easy stitch-and-flip stars add interest to the sashing. The blocks are large, measuring 10 in/26 cm when finished, so this double-bed quilt grows quickly.

Finished size: 82½ x 107½ in/214.5 x 279.5 cm

MATERIALS
All fabrics used in the quilt top are 45 in/115 cm wide, 100% cotton.

Blocks: 22 fat or long quarter yards or metres or equivalent in scraps
Sashing: white, 3½ yds/4 m
Stars and binding: red, 2¼ yds/2 m
Backing: 6½ yds/6 m in colour of your choice
Wadding: 120 x 120 in/305 x 305 cm (king size). Cotton or 80:20 cotton/polyester mix is more suitable for machine quilting. For hand quilting use either cotton/cotton blend or 2oz polyester.
Marking pencil
Machine or hand quilting thread

NOTE I started with a collection of 16 fat eighths and added more fabrics from my stash in varying amounts. In the end I used about thirty fabrics altogether, because I wanted a really scrappy look. You will need the equivalent of 768 x 3 in/8 cm squares and a fat or long quarter should yield 42 squares.

ALTERNATIVE COLOUR SCHEMES

1 A range of country fabrics has been showcased here; 2 Bright novelty fabrics add interest and an "I Spy" dimension to a child's quilt; 3 Soft pink and blue florals are used for a pretty quilt. With a more limited range of fabrics, careful placement can result in a secondary design appearing; 4 This Christmas medley is set off by plain red sashing and glittering silver stars.

1

2

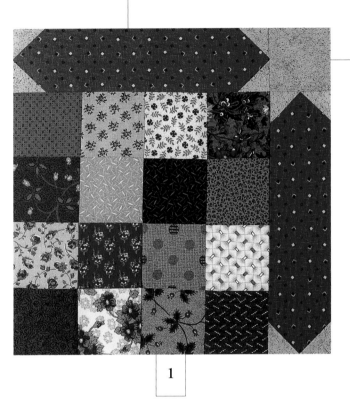

3

4

CUTTING

1 From the block fabrics, cut strips across the width of the fabric, 3 in/8 cm deep, for the 16-patch blocks. If you are cutting from long quarters, cut the strips of fabric in half so that you are working with strips measuring 3 in/8 cm x approximately 21 in/53 cm.

2 From the white sashing fabric, cut 35 strips across the width of the fabric, 3 in/8 cm deep. Cross-cut the strips into 10½ in/27.75 cm rectangles (see Note). You will need 140 rectangles. Take two of the rectangles and crosscut them to give four 3 in/8 cm squares for the outer corners of the quilt top. Cut two additional strips across the width of the fabric, 3 in/8 cm deep, and crosscut them to give 28 x 3 in/8 cm squares for use in the outer border.

NOTE If making the metric version, cut 46 strips and cut the 8 cm squares from the offcuts after cutting the 27.75 cm rectangles.

3 From the red star fabric, cut five strips across the width of the fabric, 3 in/8 cm deep. Cross-cut the strips into 63 x 3 in/8 cm squares for the centres of the stars. Cut 22 strips, 1¾ in/4.75 cm deep and cross-cut these into 504 x 1¾ in/4.75 cm squares for the star points. Cut eight strips, 2½ in/6 cm deep across the width of the remaining red fabric for the binding.

STITCHING

1 With right sides facing and taking a ¼ in/0.75 cm seam allowance, stitch the strips of fabric for the blocks into random pairs along the length of the strips. Chain piecing the strips will save time and thread. Press carefully, pressing the seam joining the strips "flat" or closed first, then flipping the top strip over and pressing from the front to ensure the seam is smooth.

2 Taking the usual seam allowance, join pairs of strips to make 32 strip sets of four fabrics with as much variety in the combinations of fabrics as possible. Press the seams as before.

3 Cut the strip sets into sections 3 in/8 cm wide (diagram 1). Each strip set should yield 6 sections.

diagram 1

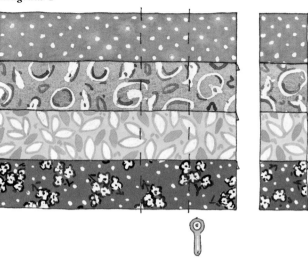

4 Taking the usual seam allowance, stitch four sections together to make a 16-patch block, which should measure 10½in/27.5 cm at this stage (diagram 2). Make 48 blocks in all. The more fabrics you have included in different combinations, the easier it will be to vary the composition of each block and achieve the scrappy look of the quilt.

diagram 2

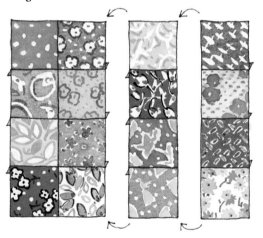

5 Prepare the sashing. Take 28 of the rectangles and four 3 in/8 cm squares of sashing fabric and set them aside for the outer border.

6 Draw a diagonal pencil line across the wrong side of each of the red 1¾ in/4.75 cm squares. Place one square on the corner of one sashing rectangle, right sides together and stitch along the drawn diagonal line. Press the square flat first to set the seam, then press the triangular flap of the square out towards the corner of the sashing rectangle: if you have stitched accurately, the triangle will fit perfectly into the corner of the sashing rectangle.

7 Trim away the excess fabric (diagram 3a), then stitch another red square on to the adjacent corner (diagram 3b). Repeat for the other two corners of the sashing rectangle, then repeat for all 110 rectangles.

diagram 3a

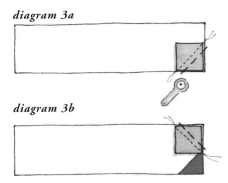

diagram 3b

8 Following the quilt plan on page 66, lay out the completed sixteen-patch blocks in eight rows of six blocks. Taking a ¼ in/0.75 cm seam allowance, stitch a sashing strip to the right-hand edge of each block and also to the left-hand edge of the first block in each row. Pin and stitch the blocks into rows and press well with the seams towards the blocks.

9 Taking the usual seam allowance, stitch six sashing strips together with a star centre square between each strip and at each end. Press the seam allowances towards the star centres. Pin the long sashing strip to fit between the first two rows of the quilt top, matching seams, and stitch carefully. Press the seam allowances towards the sashing.

10 Join the remaining rows of blocks, alternating with sashing, in the same way, and stitch a row of sashing to the top and bottom of the quilt top. Press the quilt top well.

ADDING THE BORDERS

1 The final borders will complete the stars on the outer edges of the design. Take 28 white 3 in/8 cm sashing squares and, using the same technique of stitching across the diagonal, add two small red star points to adjacent corners of each square. Press and trim away the excess fabric as before.

2 Taking a ¼ in/0.75 cm seam allowance, stitch nine of these units together with eight of the plain sashing rectangles (see quilt plan), then stitch the border to one side of the quilt, matching seams and star points as shown in the quilt assembly diagram. Repeat for the other side border.

3 Make the top and bottom border strips in the same way with the remaining 12 plain sashing rectangles alternating with the fourteen squares to which the outer star points have been added, and starting and finishing the borders with the four plain 3 in/8 cm sashing squares (diagram 4 shows a detail of the corner of the quilt). Stitch to the top and bottom of the quilt and press well with the seam allowances towards the outer borders.

diagram 4

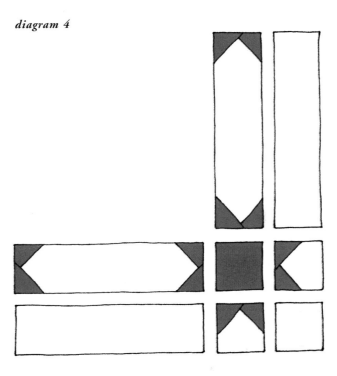

FINISHING

1 Measure the completed patchwork top and cut and piece the backing to fit with at least 2 in/5 cm all round. If you are joining the backing, don't forget to cut off the selvages as these are very tightly woven and can cause distortion in the quilt. Press the seam open.

2 Spread the backing right side down on a flat surface, then smooth out the wadding and the patchwork top, right side up, on top. Fasten together with safety pins or baste in a grid.

3 Mark the top with the desired quilting design and hand or machine quilt.

4 Join the binding strips with diagonal seams to make a continuous length to fit all around the quilt and use to bind the edges with a double-fold binding, mitred at the corners.

Tropical Fruit Sundae

Designed by Alison Wood

Luscious fruity colours in Fossil Fern fabrics glow against a plain purple background, making a quilt for a double bed that's almost good enough to eat! The half-square triangles for the flying geese border are constructed at the same time as the main blocks by stitching an extra seam, avoiding having to join any stretchy bias edges.

Finished size: 82¹⁄₂ x 106 in/212 x 274 cm

MATERIALS
All fabrics used in the quilt top are 45 in/115 cm wide, 100% cotton.

NOTE In this quilt, variety is the key and you may be able to include small amounts of lots of different fabrics from your stash.

Blocks: 12 in/30 cm of each of 20 different fabrics or equivalent in scraps. You will need 280 x 5 in/13 cm squares altogether. A 12 in/30 cm piece of fabric should yield 16 squares.

Background, first border and binding: purple, 6 yds/5.5 m

Backing: 6 yds/5.5 m in colour of your choice

Wadding: 92 x 108 in/234 x 275 cm (queen size). Cotton or 80:20 cotton/polyester mix is more suitable for machine quilting. For hand quilting use either cotton/cotton blend or 2oz polyester.

Marking pencil

Machine quilting thread

ALTERNATIVE COLOUR SCHEMES

1 Pretty pastel pinks on white are easy on the eye; 2 Reproduction fabrics on tea-dyed tone-on-tone fabrics give an antique look; 3 A variety of patterned indigo fabrics on white look crisp and minimal; 4 Bright and bold florals sparkle against turquoise to create a vibrant quilt.

1

2

3

4

CUTTING

1 From a variety of fabrics cut strips across the width of the fabric, 5 in/13 cm deep. Cross-cut the strips into 5 in/13 cm squares. You will need 280 squares.

2 From the purple background fabric cut 24 strips across the width of the fabric, 6½ in/17 cm deep. Cross-cut the strips into 6½ in/17 cm squares. You will need 140 squares.

3 From the purple background fabric cut eight strips across the width of the fabric, 4¼ in/11 cm deep, for the first border.

4 From the purple background fabric cut four strips across the width of the fabric, 2½ in/6 cm deep, for the binding.

STITCHING

1 Draw a diagonal pencil line across the wrong side of each of the 280 x 5 in/13 cm squares. Then draw a second line parallel to the diagonal line and ½ in/ 1.5 cm away from it, nearer to the corner (diagram 1).

diagram 1

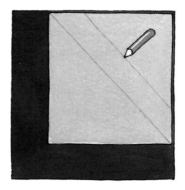

2 Place one 5 in/13 cm square on top of one 6½ in/17 cm background square, right sides together, aligning the corners. Make sure that the second marked line is nearer to the corner (see diagram 1). Repeat, until all the 140 background squares are paired up with a 5 in/13 cm square.

3 Chain piecing, stitch along the first marked diagonal line of all the paired-up squares. Snip the thread between the units.

NOTE If you have stitched accurately in step 3, the triangular flap of the smaller square, when flipped outwards, will fit perfectly into the corner of the background square. You may need to adjust your stitching slightly and sew about a needle's width inside the diagonal line – this allows for the bulk of the seam allowance.

4 Again chain piecing, stitch along the marked line nearer to the corner (diagram 2). Be careful as you guide each square through the sewing machine that it doesn't twist when you reach the edge.

diagram 2

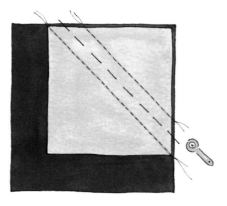

5 Snip the thread between the units and press the squares flat first to set the seams. Then press the triangular flap of the smaller square out towards the corner.

6 Flip the triangle back to enable you to cut between the two stitched lines to separate the half-square triangle unit from the main block. Repeat with the remaining blocks. Don't worry about pressing the half-square triangles open at this stage – set them aside for now.

7 Select one of the remaining 5 in/13 cm squares and place it, right sides together, on the opposite corner of one of the background squares, again checking that the inner drawn line is closer to the corner. Try to select different fabric combinations for the opposite corners, as this will give you more variety when laying out your blocks. Stitch first along the first diagonal, and then along the inner line, just as you did for the first corner (diagram 3).

diagram 3

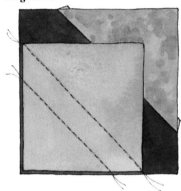

NOTE Chain piecing is efficient and saves a considerable amount of thread. It also helps avoid the cut threads being drawn down into the throat plate of the sewing machine and jamming it.

8 Snip the blocks apart and press as before, then cut between the two stitched lines. Set the half-square triangles aside for now. Each of the completed 140 blocks should measure approximately 6½ in/17 cm square. You will also have 280 half-square triangle units, each measuring approximately 4¼ in/11 cm square.

9 Following the quilt plan on page 72, lay out the completed blocks in fourteen rows of ten blocks, alternating the direction of the background trellis so that four triangle corners come together in adjacent rows to form a square on point or diamond (diagram 4). The triangles in the outer corners of the quilt "float".

diagram 4

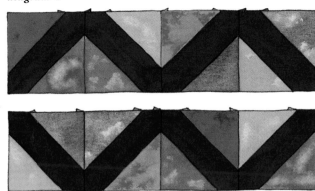

10 Taking a ¼ in/0.75 cm seam allowance, pin and stitch the blocks into rows. If you press the seams between blocks in opposite directions for alternate rows, you will be able butt them together when joining the rows, giving a neat fit in the middle of the diamond and where the diagonal trellis crosses.

NOTE Take care when sewing the blocks together into rows, as the seam allowances where the triangles meet will not butt together but lie on top of one another. It is advisable to pin, so that they do not slip out of line when stitching.

11 Taking the usual seam allowance, pin and stitch the rows together and press the top lightly.

ADDING THE BORDERS

1 Add the plain borders first. Join the eight strips of background fabric 4¼ in/11 cm wide into pairs. Measure the patchwork top through the centre from top to bottom and cut both the side borders to this length. Taking a ¼ in/0.75 cm seam allowance, pin and stitch to the sides of the quilt. Press the seams towards the borders.

2 Measure the patchwork top through the centre from side to side and cut both the top and bottom borders to this length. Taking the usual seam allowance, pin and stitch to the top and bottom of the quilt. Press as before.

3 Press the half-square triangle units open with the seam allowance towards the purple background fabric. Stitch two half-square triangle units together to make one flying geese unit, then stitch the flying geese units together to make four border strips, mixing the colours randomly (diagram 5). You will need two border strips with 18 geese units for the top and bottom of the quilt, and two border strips with 24 geese units for the sides of the quilt. You will also need 8 flying geese units for the four corner squares on point.

diagram 5

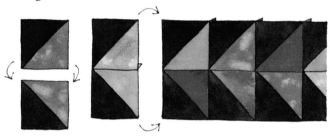

NOTE This makes a total of 92 geese from 184 half-square triangle units. You can use the remaining 96 half-square triangle units to make cushions or pillows, or incorporate them into another quilt.

4 Following the quilt plan on page 72 for the direction of the geese and for the position of the corner units, pin and stitch the flying geese border strips first to the sides of the patchwork top, then to the top and bottom. Take particular care when stitching them in place that you do not stretch the pieced edges. Press the seams towards the plain borders.

FINISHING

1 Measure the completed patchwork top and cut and piece the backing to fit with at least 2 in/5 cm extra on all sides. If you are joining the backing, don't forget to cut off the selvages as these are very tightly woven and can cause distortion in the quilt. Press the seam open.

2 Spread the backing right side down on a flat surface, then smooth out the wadding and the patchwork top, right side up, on top. Fasten together with safety pins or baste in a grid.

3 Machine quilt in-the-ditch along the seams forming the edge of the diamond blocks, along the construction lines between the blocks, and around the flying geese. To finish, quilt triangles to echo the flying geese in the plain borders. This provides a grid of machine quilting that secures the layers without the need for marking, except in the plain borders.

4 Join the binding strips with diagonal seams to make a continuous length to fit all around the quilt and use to bind the edges with a double-fold binding, mitred at the corners.

All Churned Up

Designed by Sarah Wellfair

I've used two contrasting colours in the "Churn Dash" block to accentuate the pattern. I've then used a floral print which combines these two colours to soften the overall effect. The large plain squares and wide borders ensure that the pieced top for this king-size bed is quickly made. For a smaller bed, you could either leave off one of the borders or make both narrower.

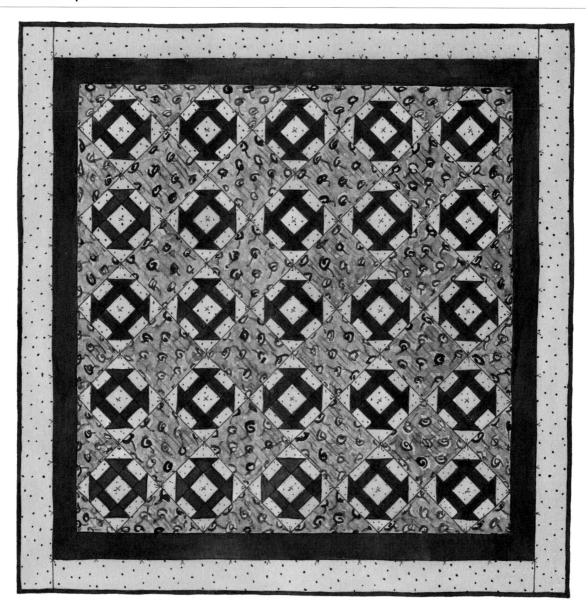

Finished size: 105½ x 105½ in/264 x 264 cm

MATERIALS
All fabrics used in the quilt top are 45 in/115 cm
wide, 100% cotton

Blue fabric for Churn Dash blocks: 2 yds/1.75 m
Cream fabric for Churn Dash blocks: 2½ yds/2.25 m
For plain blocks: 3½ yds/3.25 m of blue/cream roses
fabric
Inner border: 1¾ yds/1.5 m extra of the blue fabric

Outer border: 2¼ yds/2 m extra of the cream fabric
Backing: 3⅜ yds/3 m of 120 in/305 cm wide fabric or
10 yds/9 m of 45 in/115 cm wide fabric in colour of
your choice
Wadding: 120 x 120 in/305 x 305 cm
Binding: 1¼ yds/1 m extra of the blue/cream roses
fabric
Marking pencil and ruler
Thread for ties: perle cotton in blue and cream

ALTERNATIVE COLOUR SCHEMES

1 Pastel pink and a small floral print make a very pretty quilt; 2 Purple is the dominant colour here, softened by the large floral print; 3 Light and dark floral prints make a lively pattern; 4 Two mellow brown prints create a warm and cozy look.

1

2

3

4

CUTTING

1   From the blue fabric, cut seven strips across the width of the fabric, $4^7/_8$ in/12.5 cm deep. Cross-cut the strips into 50 squares, $4^7/_8$ x $4^7/_8$ in/12.5 x 12.5 cm.

2   From the cream fabric, cut seven strips across the width of the fabric, $4^7/_8$ in/12.5 cm deep. Cross-cut the strips into 50 squares, $4^7/_8$ x $4^7/_8$ in/12.5 x 12.5 cm.

3   From each of the remaining blue and cream fabrics, cut twelve strips across the width of the fabric, $2^1/_2$ in/6 cm deep.

4   From the remaining cream fabric, cut three strips across the width of the fabric, $4^1/_2$ in/11.5 cm deep. Cross-cut the strips into 25 squares, $4^1/_2$ x $4^1/_2$ in/ 11.5 x 11.5 cm.

5   From the cream/blue roses fabric, cut six strips across the width of the fabric, $12^1/_2$ in/31.5 cm deep. Cross-cut the strips into 16 squares, $12^1/_2$ x $12^1/_2$ in/ 31.5 x 31.5 cm.

6   From the cream/blue roses fabric, cut four squares, $18^1/_4$ x $18^1/_4$ in/46 x 46 cm and cross-cut these into four triangles by cutting across both diagonals (total of 16 side triangles).

7   From the cream/blue roses fabric, cut two squares, $9^3/_8$ x $9^3/_8$ in/23.75 x 23.75 cm and cross-cut these into two triangles each by cutting across one diagonal (total of four corner triangles).

8   From the blue inner border fabric, cut nine strips across the width of the fabric, 5 in/12.5 cm deep. From the cream outer border fabric, cut ten strips across the width of the fabric, $6^1/_2$ in/16.5 cm deep.

9   If using 45 in/115 cm wide backing fabric, cut it across the width of the fabric into three equal lengths.

10   For the binding, cut 11 strips of fabric, $2^1/_2$ in/ 6 cm deep, across the width of the fabric, to make up a 455 in/1130 cm length.

STITCHING

1   Using a marking pencil and ruler, draw a diagonal line across the wrong side of each of the 50 cream $4^7/_8$ in/12.5 cm squares.

2   Take one cream square and one matching blue square and place right sides together. Stitch $1/_4$ in/ 0.75 cm on both sides of the marked line (diagram 1). Repeat with the remaining cream and blue $4^7/_8$ in/ 12.5 cm squares (total of 50 stitched squares).

diagram 1

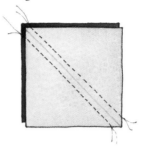

3   Press each stitched pair of squares flat to set the seams, then cut across the diagonal to make two half square triangle units. Press the seam allowance of each unit towards the blue fabric. Trim off the small "ears" of fabric that extend beyond the square (total of 100 half square triangle units) (diagram 2).

diagram 2

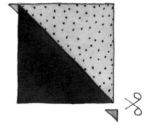

4   Take one cream and one blue $2^1/_2$ in/6 cm strip and place right sides together. Taking a $1/_4$ in/0.75 cm seam allowance, stitch along one long side.

5   Open out the strips and press the seam allowance towards the blue strip. Repeat with the remaining blue and cream strips.

6   Cross-cut the strips into 100 squares, $4^1/_2$ x $4^1/_2$ in/ 11.5 x 11.5 cm (diagram 3).

diagram 3

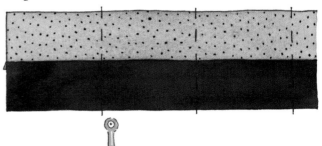

7 To make the first Churn Dash block, lay out the pieced squares and the cream $4^{1}/_{2}$ in/11.5 cm square in the correct order (diagram 4). Taking a $^{1}/_{4}$ in/ 0.75 cm seam allowance, stitch them together in three rows. On rows 1 and 3, press the seams towards the centre block. On row 2, press the seams away from the centre.

diagram 4

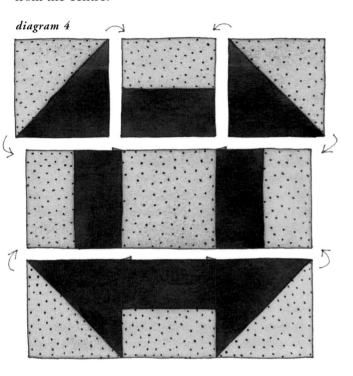

8 Pin and stitch the rows together, matching seams carefully. Repeat to make a total of 25 blocks.

9 Taking the usual seam allowance, pin and stitch the blocks in diagonal rows, alternating Churn Dash

diagram 5

blocks with background blocks and adding the side and corner triangles as you work (diagram 5). Refer to the quilt plan on page 80 for the correct number of blocks in each row. Press the seams towards the background blocks. Pin and stitch the rows together, matching the seams.

ADDING THE BORDERS

1 Join the 5 in/12.5 cm strips of blue inner border fabric together to make one long piece and cut the inner borders from this. Join the $6^{1}/_{2}$ in/16.5 cm strips of cream outer border fabric together to make one long piece and cut the outer borders from this.

2 Measure the pieced top through the centre from side to side, then cut two strips of the inner border fabric to this measurement. Taking a $^{1}/_{4}$ in/0.75 cm seam allowance, pin and stitch to the top and bottom of the quilt.

3 Measure the pieced top through the centre from top to bottom, then cut two strips of the inner border fabric to this measurement. Taking a $^{1}/_{4}$ in/0.75 cm seam allowance, pin and stitch to the sides.

4 Repeat steps 2 and 3 using the outer border fabric.

FINISHING

1 Join the backing pieces if necessary. Measure the finished patchwork top, add 2 in/5 cm to each side and cut the backing and wadding to this size.

2 Spread the backing right side down on a flat surface, then smooth out the wadding and the patchwork top, right side up, on top. Fasten together with safety pins or baste in a grid.

3 Quilt as desired. I have tied the quilt using perle cotton thread in a contrasting colour to the fabric, placing the ties in the centres and points of the blocks and at regular intervals down both sides of the inner border.

4 Trim off any excess wadding and backing so they are even with the quilt top. Join the binding strips with diagonal seams to make a continuous length to fit all round the quilt and use to bind the edges with a double-fold binding, mitred at the corners.

Lavender Mist

Designed by Eilean MacDonald

This enchanting queen-size quilt is perfectly at home in a contemporary or a traditional setting and is simplicity itself to make. It is an ideal quilt for beginners to perfect their sewing and colour theory skills.

Finished size: 89 x 110½ in/221 x 275 cm

MATERIALS
All fabrics used in the quilt top are 45 in/115 cm wide, 100% cotton.

Purple fabric: 3 yds/2.8 m
Lilac fabric: 3¾ yds/3.5 m

Blue fabric: 3¾ yds/3.5 m
Backing: 2⅝ yds/2.4 m, 110 in/279 cm wide, in colour of your choice
Wadding: low loft 100% cotton, 92 x 114 in/ 233 x 287 cm
Invisible machine thread
Binding: random strips of the above fabrics

ALTERNATIVE COLOUR SCHEMES

1 Using fabrics with bold floral designs and gold detail paired with a muted busy fabric, gives a rich alternative; 2 The use of autumnal red, yellow and brown fabrics makes a warm and wonderful quilt for winter; 3 Using grey and beige prints with plain black would look dramatic in a neutral-toned bedroom; 4 Combining purple and green print fabrics with plain pale green creates an old-fashioned quilt with an antique look.

1

2

3

4

CUTTING

1 From the purple fabric, cut 80 squares, 5¹/₂ x 5¹/₂ in/14 x 14 cm.

2 From the lilac fabric, cut 120 squares, 5¹/₂ x 5¹/₂ in/14 x 14 cm.

3 From the blue fabric, cut 120 squares, 5¹/₂ x 5¹/₂ in/14 x 14 cm.

4 For the borders, cut and piece fabric as follows:
two blue strips, 3¹/₂ x 97 in/9 x 241 cm
two blue strips, 3¹/₂ x 85 in/9 x 210 cm
two lilac strips, 3¹/₂ x 104 in/9 x 258 cm
two lilac strips, 3¹/₂ x 91 in/9 x 227 cm
two purple strips, 2 x 110 in/5 x 274 cm
two purple strips, 3¹/₂ x 95 in/9 x 235 cm.

5 For the binding, cut enough random strips of each fabric, 2¹/₂ in/6 cm deep, to make up a 400 in/ 1016 cm length.

STITCHING

1 Draw a light pencil line diagonally across the wrong side of two of the lilac squares. With right sides together, place the two lilac squares on top of two purple squares. Stitch a ¹/₄ in/0.75 cm seam on either side of marked pencil line (diagram 1).

diagram 1

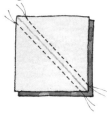

2 Press the seams flat to set them, then cut the squares apart along the pencil line to form four lilac/purple half-square triangle units. Press the units open, with the seam allowance pressed towards the darker fabric.

3 Repeat with two blue and two purple squares to make four blue/purple half-square triangle units, and with four blue and four lilac squares to make eight blue/lilac half-square triangle units.

4 To make one block, arrange the half-square triangle units as shown in diagram 2. Taking a ¹/₄ in/0.75 cm seam allowance, stitch them together in

strips of four. Press the seams to the left or right on alternate rows, so that the seams will butt together neatly when the rows are joined.

diagram 2

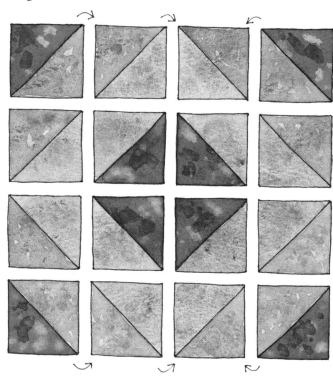

5 Taking the usual seam allowance and matching the seams carefully, pin and stitch the four rows together to complete the block (diagram 3).

diagram 3

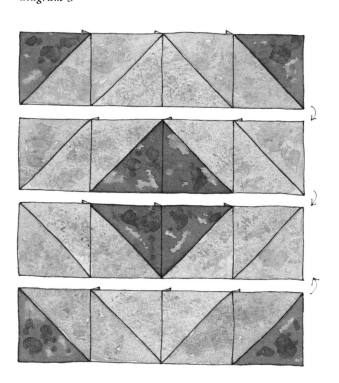

ADDING THE BORDERS

1　Taking a ¼ in/0.75 cm seam allowance, pin and stitch the two longer blue borders to the sides of the quilt. Press the seams towards the borders. Trim the length of the borders to fit (diagram 4).

diagram 4

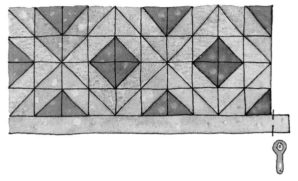

2　Taking the usual seam allowance, pin and stitch the two shorter blue borders to the top and bottom of the quilt. Press the seams towards the outer edge. Trim the length of the borders to fit.

3　Repeat steps 1 and 2 to attach the lilac borders.

4　Repeat steps 1 and 2 to attach the purple borders.

FINISHING

1　Spread the backing right side down on a flat surface, then smooth out the wadding and the patchwork top, right side up, on top. Fasten together with safety pins or baste in a grid.

2　Using invisible machine thread, quilt in-the-ditch around each coloured square and between the borders.

3　Trim off any excess wadding and backing, so they are even with the quilt top. Stitch the random binding strips with diagonal seams to make a continuous length to fit all around the quilt and use to bind the edges with a double-fold binding, mitred at the corners.

6　Repeat steps 1 to 5 until you have made a total of 20 blocks.

7　Following the quilt plan on page 86, lay out the blocks in five rows of four blocks. Taking a ¼ in/ 0.75 cm seam allowance and matching seams, pin and stitch the blocks together. Press the seams between blocks to the left or right on alternate rows, so that the seams will butt together neatly at the next stage.

8　Taking the usual seam allowance and matching the seams, pin and stitch the five rows together. Press the seams open.

Medallion Magic

Designed by Judi Mendelssohn

At first glance this queen-size quilt has the appearance of a medallion quilt with a central diamond, but it is actually very simply put together in diagonal rows. It could be extended to fit a king-size bed by adding borders.

Finished size: 86 x 104 in/218 x 264 cm

MATERIALS

All fabrics used in the quilt top are 45 in/115 cm
wide, 100% cotton.

Big flower print: 2 yds/1.9 m
Small black print: 1½ yds/1.4 m
Small cream print: 1½ yds/1.4 m

Pale pink: 1 yd/1 m
Contrast darker pink: 1 yd/1 m
Creamy flower print: 2¼ yds/1.9 m
Binding: An extra 27 in/80 cm of the creamy flower
print
Wadding: 90 x 108 in/229 x 274 cm
Backing: 6 yds/5.5 m in colour of your choice
Quilting thread

ALTERNATIVE COLOUR SCHEMES

1 A combination of black and white with red accents makes a dramatic colour scheme for a modern interior; 2 Beautiful Bali fabrics make a harmonious design; 3 The traditional pairing of blue and white is given further impact by the addition of orange highlights; 4 Yellow, green and blue fabrics give a bright, summery look to the quilt.

CUTTING

1   From the big flower print, cut ten strips, 6½ in/16.5 cm deep, across the width of the fabric. Cross-cut into 57 squares, 6½ x 6½ in/16.5 x 16.5 cm.

2   From each of the small black print fabric and the small cream print fabric, cut eleven-and-a-half strips, 3½ in/9 cm deep, across the width of the fabric.

3   From the pale pink fabric, cut five strips, 6½ in/16.5 cm deep, across the width of the fabric. Cross-cut into 30 squares, 6½ x 6½ in/16.5 x 16.5 cm.

4   From the contrast darker pink fabric, cut five strips, 6½ in/16.5 cm deep, across the width of the fabric. Cross-cut into 28 squares, 6½ x 6½ in/ 16.5 x 16.5 cm.

5   From the creamy flower print fabric, cut six strips, 6½ in/16.5 cm deep, across the width of the fabric. Cross-cut into 36 squares, 6½ x 6½ in/16.5 x 16.5 cm.

6   From the remaining creamy flower print fabric, cut three strips, 9¾ in/24.5 cm deep, across the width of the fabric. Cut into ten squares, 9¾ x 9¾ in/ 24.5 x 24.5 cm. Cut these into 40 quarter-square triangles to form the side triangles of the quilt. Trim the remaining half-strip down to 5¼ in/13.5 cm deep. Cut into two squares, 5¼ x 5¼ in/13.5 x 13.5 cm. Cut these into four half-square triangles to form the corner triangles of the quilt.

7   From the creamy flower print fabric for the binding, cut nine strips, 2¾ in/7 cm deep, across the width of the fabric.

8   Cut the backing across the width of the fabric into two equal lengths.

STITCHING

1   Place a strip of small black print fabric right sides together with a strip of small cream print fabric. Stitch together down one long edge, taking a ¼ in/0.75 cm seam allowance. Press the seams towards the small black print fabric. Repeat with the remaining strips in these colours.

2   Cross-cut the strips into 136 segments, 3½ in/9 cm wide (diagram 1a). Take two matching pairs and pin right sides together, reversing the colours and

matching the centre seams. Taking the usual seam allowance, stitch together into 68 four-patch blocks (diagram 1b)

diagram 1a

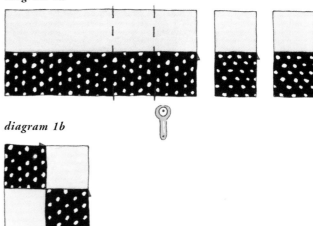

diagram 1b

3   Follow the quilt plan on page 92 for the correct number of blocks in each row and the correct orientation of the triangles. Pin and stitch the four-patch blocks and the plain blocks together in diagonal rows, adding the side and corner triangles as you work and taking the usual seam allowance (diagram 2). Press the seams on either side of the squares to opposite sides on alternate rows, so that when you join the rows, the seams will butt together well.

diagram 2

4   Taking the usual seam allowance, pin and stitch the rows together, matching the seams carefully.

NOTE When you join the blocks, press the seam allowances towards the big flower print squares first to establish a sequence across each row.

FINISHING

1 Cut the selvages from the backing fabric and, taking a ¹/₂ in/1.5 cm seam allowance, stitch the two lengths of fabric together along the trimmed edges. Press the seam open.

2 Spread the backing right side down on a flat surface, then smooth out the wadding and the patch-work top, right side up, on the top. Fasten together with safety pins or baste in a grid.

3 Quilt in the pattern of your choice. I have quilted in-the-ditch round the on-point squares formed by the four-patch blocks.

4 Stitch two of the binding strips together for the top and bottom of the quilt. Stitch two-and-a-half of the binding strips together for the sides of the quilt. Fold the strips in half lengthways to create a double binding.

5 Trim off any excess wadding and backing so they are even with the quilt top. Place the longer binding strips along the sides of the quilt, aligning raw edges. Pin in place and stitch, taking a ¹/₄ in/0.75 cm seam allowance. Turn the binding over to the back of the quilt. Slip stitch in place using a matching thread.

6 Turn under the raw edges at each end of the shorter binding strips. Stitch to the top and bottom of the quilt as above.

Revolutions

Designed by Gail Smith

The inspiration for this queen-size quilt came from my fascination with geometric shapes. I just thought "What if?" and allowed various block arrangements to come into my mind. The one shown here is so simple, yet very effective, employing clever use of colour and shape. It is assembled and quilted in two halves to make the quilting easier.

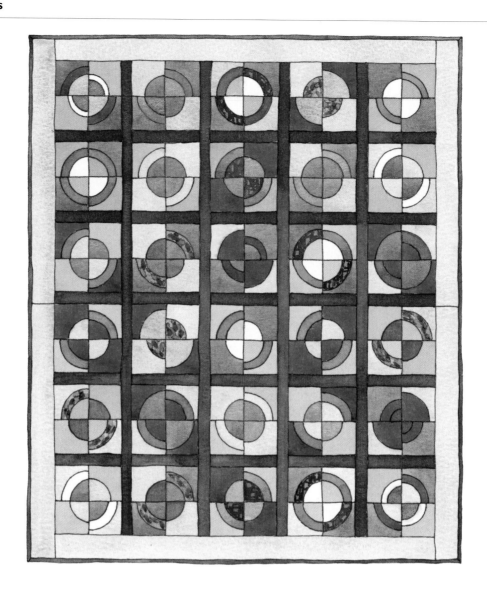

Finished size: 95 x 112¹/₂ in/234 x 277 cm

MATERIALS

All fabrics used in the quilt top are 45 in/115 cm wide, 100% cotton.

For the block backgrounds:

2¹/₄ yds/2 m of lilac (or 1¹/₈ yds/1 m of two different lilacs)

2¹/₄ yds/2 m of deep sky blue (or 1¹/₈ yds/1 m of two different blues)

4 yds/3.5 m of mid green (can be mixed as above)

1 yd/1 m of pale green

For the 12¹/₂ in/32 cm circles:

28 in/70 cm of jade green

28 in/70 cm of deep sky blue

Fat quarter of turquoise (22 x 18 in/56 x 50 cm)

14 in/35 cm of cerise pink

1¹/₈ yds/1 m of purple

14 in/35cm of ivory

For the 9¹/₂ in/24 cm circles:

10 in/25 cm of jade green

10 in/25cm of deep sky blue

20 in/50 cm of lilac

10 in/25cm of turquoise

20 in/50 cm of cerise pink

20 in/50 cm of purple

20 in/50 cm of ivory

Sashing: 3¹/₂ yds/3 m of dark purple

Border: 3 yds/3 m of pale green

Backing: 8 yds/7.5 m of 45 in/115 cm wide fabric or 5¹/₂ yds/5 m of 60 in/150 cm wide fabric in colour of your choice

Wadding: 120 x 120 in/305 x 305 cm

Binding: 28 in/70 cm fabric in contrasting colour

Matching threads for piecing

Variegated cotton quilting thread

ALTERNATIVE COLOUR SCHEMES

1 Pastel colours lend themselves well to this design, where the tiny flower prints and the brighter pink add interest; 2 Mustard, gold and burgundy make a bold, but warm colour scheme, ideal for people who like autumn colours; 3 A soft colour scheme using cream, brown with a hint of metallic gold and other colours would make a good wedding or golden anniversary quilt; 4 Gorgeous aquas, blues and greens used together are reminiscent of the deep blue sea.

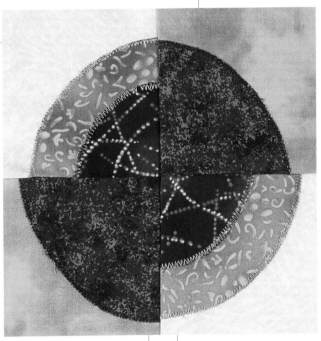

1

2

3

4

CUTTING

Follow the quilt plan on page 98 for the placement of the squares and circles and cut out the fabrics accordingly. Alternatively, make your own colour plan before you start or arrange the colours randomly.

1   From the block background fabrics, cut 30 squares, 16 x 16 in/40 x 40 cm.

2   From the fabric for the larger circles, cut circles, 12½ in/32 cm in diameter as follows: 4 jade green, 6 deep sky blue, 1 turquoise, 2 cerise pink, 8 purple, 2 ivory.

3   From the fabric for the smaller circles, cut circles 9½ in/24 cm in diameter as follows:
2 jade green, 2 deep sky blue, 5 lilac, 4 turquoise, 5 cerise pink, 6 purple, 4 ivory.

NOTE   Plates or pizza bases of a suitable size are ideal to use as templates when marking the circles on to the fabric. Alternatively, use a pair of compasses or the string and pencil method.

4   From the dark purple sashing fabric, first cut four long vertical strips down the length of fabric, 3 in/7.5 cm wide. From the remaining dark purple fabric, cut 13 strips across the width of the fabric, 3 in/7.5 cm deep. Cut these in half, as you will need 25 strips, 16 in/40 cm long.

5   From the pale green border fabric, cut six strips down the length of the fabric, 5½ in/14 cm wide. This gives you three strips for each half of the quilt.

6   If using 45 in/115 cm wide backing fabric, cut it widthways into three equal lengths. Cut one length in half lengthways and stitch one half to each of the other two lengths. These will now be big enough to back the two halves of the quilt. Alternatively, if using 60 in/150 cm fabric, cut it in half widthways.

7   From the contrasting fabric, cut 10 strips across the width of the fabric, 2½ in/6 cm deep, for the binding.

STITCHING

1   Find the centres of the squares and the circles by pressing them in half and in half again with your iron set on cotton. When you open them out, you will see the centre creases.

2   Matching the centre points, place the circles on to the squares, following the quilt plan or your own arrangement. Use either a single circle or place a smaller circle on top of a larger one. Pin around the edge of the circles with the pins pointing outwards (diagram 1).

diagram 1

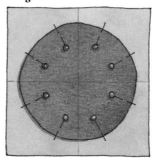

3   Set your machine to a zig-zag stitch and, using a matching thread, stitch around each circle until you have completed 30 blocks. You may find that the blocks have distorted slightly, so press them lightly on the reverse to help them lie flat.

4   Following the quilt plan or your own design, sort the blocks into pairs ready to create new blocks.

5   Working with the first sorted pair, cut each block in half, then rotate the halves and cut again, forming quarters (diagram 2).

diagram 2

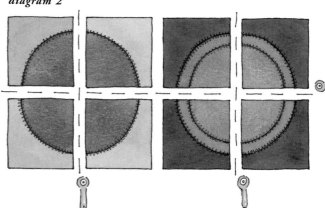

6 Swap two units of each block with two units from its partner, forming two identical new blocks. Taking a ¼ in/0.75 cm seam allowance, pin and stitch the units together in pairs. Press the seams open. Then, matching the seams, stitch the pairs together to form the new blocks. Press the seams open (diagram 3).

diagram 3

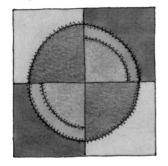

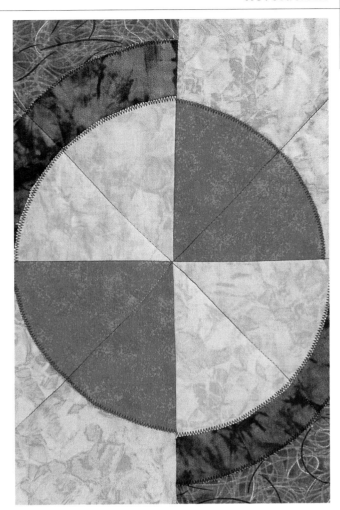

7 Repeat steps 5 and 6 until you have 30 blocks. Lay them out in six rows of five blocks, following the quilt plan on page 98 or until you are happy with the placement of the colours and shapes. Cut up small pieces of paper, number them 1-30 and pin them near the top of each block – this will help keep them in order when you attach the sashing.

8 Taking a ¼ in/0.75 cm seam allowance, pin and stitch short lengths of sashing in between the blocks (diagram 4). Join blocks 1-15 first, then blocks 16-30 and keep these as two separate units. Add sashing strips to the bottom of blocks 1-15 but not to the bottom of blocks 26-30. Press the seams towards the dark fabric.

9 Lining up the blocks carefully and double checking as you go, pin the long sashing strips between the vertical rows (diagram 5). Taking the usual seam allowance, stitch the sashing to the blocks. Press the seams towards the dark fabric.

diagram 4

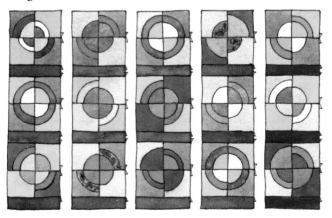

diagram 5

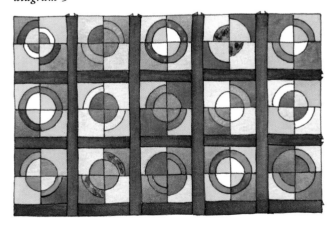

ADDING THE BORDERS

1 Add the borders to each half of the quilt separately, as follows. Measure the upper half (1-15) through the centre from side to side, then cut one of the 5½ in/14 cm pale green strips to this measurement. Taking a ¼ in/0.75 cm seam allowance, pin and stitch to the top. Measure the upper half through the centre from top to bottom, then cut two of the 5½ in/14 cm pale green strips to this measurement. Pin and stitch to the sides of the quilt.

2 Repeat for the lower half of the quilt (16-30), stitching the border first to the bottom and then to the sides of the quilt. Press the seams towards the darker side.

FINISHING

1 Cut out two pieces of wadding, approximately 2 in/5 cm wider all round than the quilt halves. For each half, spread the backing right side down on a flat surface, then smooth out the wadding and the patchwork top, right side up, on top. Fasten together with safety pins or baste in a grid.

2 Quilt the blocks of the two units as shown in diagram 6 but do not quilt the border at this stage. Ensure that you leave at least ½ in/1.5 cm unquilted between the two units so that they can be joined after quilting. Also, do not trim the wadding and backing too close at this stage.

3 When the quilting of the main sections is complete, place the two halves of the quilt together with right sides facing, matching seams. Pin and tack just the pieced layer along the centre seam, without catching in the wadding or backing. Taking a ¼ in/0.75 cm seam allowance, machine stitch along the centre seam, supporting the weight of the quilt as you work.

4 Place the quilt right side down on a flat surface. Bring the edges of the wadding together and carefully trim it along the centre seam so that it butts up neatly. Join the wadding by hand. Turn under the raw edges of the backing fabric along the centre seam, trimming them first if necessary, and slip stitch together to make a neat join.

5 Trim off any excess wadding and backing around the edges so that they are even with the quilt top. Now quilt the plain green border with a continuous wavy line as shown in diagram 6, leaving ½ in/1.5 cm unquilted at the edges for the binding.

6 Join the binding strips with diagonal seams to make a continuous length to fit all round the quilt and use to bind the edges with a double-fold binding, mitred at the corners.

diagram 6

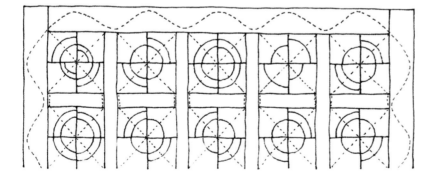

Simply Chevrons

Designed by Sarah Wellfair

Strip-piecing and an easy method for stitching the two halves of the block together ensure that this quilt for a king-size bed is quickly and accurately assembled. For a smaller bed, you could either leave off the second border or make both borders narrower.

Finished size: 108 x 108 in/274 x 274 cm

MATERIALS
All fabrics used in the quilt top are 45 in/115 cm wide, 100% cotton

For chevrons: 1¹⁄₈ yds/1 m each of four different print fabrics in green, salmon, crimson and black
For alternate squares and setting triangles: 4¹⁄₂ yds/ 4 m of cream print fabric

Inner border: 1³⁄₄ yds/1.5 m extra of the crimson print fabric
Outer border: 1³⁄₄ yds/1.5 m extra of the salmon print fabric
Backing: 3³⁄₈ yds/3 m of 120 in/305 cm wide fabric or 10 yds/9 m of 45 in/115 cm wide fabric in colour of your choice
Wadding: 120 x 120 in/305 x 305 cm
Binding: 1¹⁄₄ yds/1 m extra of the black print fabric
Thread for ties: perle cotton in crimson and salmon

ALTERNATIVE COLOUR SCHEMES

1 Pastel stripes and florals make a summery colour scheme; 2 Blues and cream have a more masculine appeal; 3 Batik dyed fabrics are perfect for this block, producing a harmonious colour scheme; 4 Mixing large and small florals with spotted prints gives a really lively design.

CUTTING

1 Trim each piece of fabric for the chevrons to 43 in/106.5 cm wide. From each fabric piece, cut 14 strips across the width of the fabric, 2½ in/6.5 cm deep.

2 From the cream print fabric, cut 49 squares, 8½ x 8½ in/21.5 x 21.5 cm for the alternate squares.

3 From the cream print fabric, cut thirteen 12 in/30.5 cm squares and cross-cut these into four triangles by cutting across both diagonals (you need a total of 49 side triangles).

4 From the cream print fabric, cut two 6¼ in/ 15.5 cm squares and cross-cut these into two triangles each by cutting across one diagonal (total of four corner triangles).

5 From the crimson inner border fabric, cut nine strips across the width of the fabric, 6 in/15 cm deep. From the salmon outer border fabric, cut ten strips across the width of the fabric, 5½ in/14 cm deep.

6 If using 45 in/115 cm wide backing fabric, cut it across the width of the fabric into three equal lengths.

7 For the binding, cut 11 strips of fabric, 2 ½ in/ 6 cm deep, across the width of the fabric.

STITCHING

1 Take one strip of each of the chevron colours and, taking a ¼ in/0.75 cm seam allowance, stitch the strips together along their long edges to make the first unit in the order: green, crimson, salmon, black (diagram 1). The unit should now measure 8½ x 42 in/21.5 cm x 106.5 cm.

diagram 1

2 Repeat step 1 to make eight of these units. Take half the units and press the seams towards the bottom strip. Place the pressed units in a pile to one side.

3 Take the remaining units and press the seams towards the top strip. Place the units in a separate pile.

4 Take one unit from each pile and place them right sides together, matching the seams carefully. (As the seams are pressed in opposite directions, they should lock together when you come to stitch the chevrons in step 6.) Trim off one side edge to straighten it, then cut five squares 8½ x 8½ in/21.5 x 21.5 cm (diagram 2).

diagram 2

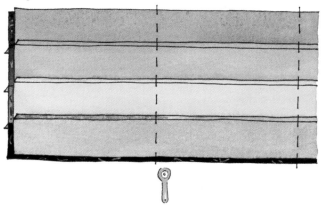

5 You will now be working in pairs of squares, so keep each pair together. Complete one set of chevrons before going on to cut and stitch the remaining units – this should stop them getting mixed up.

6 Cut the first pair of squares in half on the diagonal to form two pairs of triangles. Take one pair of triangles and keep them firmly together, so that the seams remain aligned. Taking a ¼ in/0.75 cm seam allowance, pin and stitch along the diagonal edge. Repeat with the other pair of triangles (diagram 3). Each pair of squares will give you two chevron blocks in reversed colour order.

diagram 3

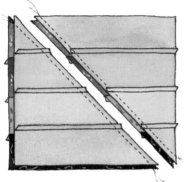

7 Repeat steps 1 to 6 with the remaining fabric strips until you have made 64 chevrons in total.

8 Following the quilt plan on page 106, lay out the blocks in diagonal rows, alternating chevron blocks with background blocks and adding the side and corner triangles as you work (diagram 4). Then, taking a ¼ in/0.75 cm seam allowance, pin and stitch the blocks together in rows, matching seams carefully. Press the seams towards the plain blocks.

diagram 4

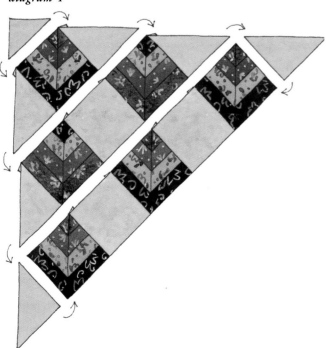

9 Taking the usual seam allowance, pin and stitch the rows together, matching the seams carefully.

ADDING THE BORDERS

1 Join the 6 in/15 cm strips of crimson inner border fabric together to make one long piece and cut the inner borders from this as described below. Join the 5½ in/14 cm strips of salmon outer border fabric together to make one long piece and cut the outer borders from this as described below.

2 Measure the pieced top through the centre from side to side, then cut two strips of the inner border fabric to this measurement. Taking a ¼ in/0.75 cm seam allowance, pin and stitch to the top and bottom of the quilt.

3 Measure the pieced top through the centre from top to bottom, then cut two strips of the inner border fabric to this measurement. Taking the usual seam allowance, pin and stitch to the sides.

4 Repeat steps 2 and 3 using the outer border fabric.

FINISHING

1 Join the backing pieces. Measure the finished patchwork top, add 2 in/5 cm to each side and cut the backing and wadding to this size.

2 Spread the backing right side down on a flat surface, then smooth out the wadding and the patchwork top, right side up, on top. Fasten together with safety pins or baste in a grid.

3 Quilt as desired. Using the perle cotton, I tied each block in the centre and placed ties at regular intervals down the centre of both borders. I used salmon thread for the unpieced squares and outer border and crimson for chevron blocks and inner border.

4 Trim off any excess wadding and backing so they are even with the quilt top. Join the binding strips with diagonal seams to make a continuous length to fit all round the quilt and use to bind the edges with a double-fold binding, mitred at the corners.

THE CONTRIBUTORS

Jane Coombes is a patchwork and quilting tutor and is a member of the teaching team at Creative Quilting near Hampton Court in Surrey.

Nikki Foley has a HNC in interior design and uses this to her advantage when designing quilts and patterns for her business 'The Sewing Shed': www.thesewingshed@aol.com

Janet Goddard writes patterns for magazines and books and teaches patchwork across Hertfordshire, Essex and North London.

Katharine Guerrier is a leading quilt designer, who frequently exhibits in national shows. She is also the author of a number of books on quilt techniques.

Gwen Jones is largely self taught and loves all forms of needle-work but particularly patchwork and quilting. Currently chair-woman of her local quilting group, she is also involved with other quilting groups.

Eilean MacDonald studied for a BA (Hons) in Contemporary Textile Practice at the University of Wales Institute, Cardiff and now undertakes private commissions for her textured textile creations.

Judi Mendelssohn's work is on permanent display as a member of the Makers Guild In Wales at 'Craft in the Bay' in Cardiff, and she gives talks and workshops in patchwork all over the country.

Gail Smith opened her shop, "Abigail Crafts", after completing a City and Guild course; she is a qualified adult education teacher, running local patchwork groups.

Sarah Wellfair is a qualified teacher who runs a full programme of workshops from her patchwork shop, Goose Chase Quilting, at Leckhampton in Gloucestershire.

Alison Wood teaches classes and works part-time at The Quilt Room in Dorking, Surrey.

SUPPLIERS

UK

Abigail Crafts
3-5 Regent Street
Stonehouse
Gloucestershire GL10 2AA
Tel: 01453 823691
www.abigailcrafts.co.uk
Patchwork and embroidery
supplies

The Bramble Patch
West Street
Weedon
Northants NN7 4QU
Tel: 01327 342212
Patchwork and quilting
supplies

Custom Quilting Limited
"Beal na Tra"
Derrymihan West
Castletownbere
Co Cork, Eire
Email: patches@iol.ie
Longarm quilting services

The Cotton Patch
1285 Stratford Road
Hall Green
Birmingham B28 9AJ
Tel: 0121 702 2840
Patchwork and quilting
supplies

Creative Quilting
3 Bridge Road
East Molesey
Surrey KT8 9EU
Tel: 020 8941 7075
Specialist retailer

Fred Aldous Ltd
PO Box 135
37 Lever Street
Manchester M1 1LW
Tel: 0161 236 2477
Mail order craft materials

Frome Valley Quilting
335 Church Road
Frampton Cotterell
Bristol BS36 2AB
Tel: 01454 880880
Email:
rosemary@frome-valley.co.uk
Longarm quilting services

Goose Chase Quilting
65 Great Norwood Street
Leckhampton
Cheltenham GL50 2BQ
Tel: 01242 512639
Patchwork and quilting
supplies

Hab-bits
Unit 9, Vale Business Park
Cowbridge
Vale of Glamorgan
CF71 7PF
Tel: 01446 775150
Haberdashery supplies

Patchwork Direct
c/o Heirs & Graces
King Street
Bakewell
Derbyshire DE45 1DZ
Tel: 01629 815873
www.patchworkdirect.com
Patchwork and quilting
supplies

Purely Patchwork
23 High Street
Linlithgow
West Lothian
Scotland
Tel: 01506 846200
Patchwork and quilting
supplies

The Quilt Loft
9/10 Havercroft Buildings
North Street
Worthing
West Sussex BN11 1DY
Tel: 01903 233771
Quilt supplies, classes and
workshops

The Quilt Room
20 West Street
Dorking
Surrey RH4 1BL
Tel: 01306 740739
www.quiltroom.co.uk
Quilt supplies, classes and
workshops
Mail order: The Quilt Room
c/o Carvilles
Station Road
Dorking
Surrey RH4 1XH
Tel: 01306 877307

Quilting Solutions
Firethorn
Rattlesden Road
Drinkstone
Bury St Edmunds
Suffolk IP30 9TL
Tel: 01449 735280
Email: firethorn@lineone.net
www.quiltingsolutions.co.uk
Longarm quilting services

The Sewing Shed
Shanahill West
Keel
Castlemaine
Co Kerry, Eire
Tel: 00 353 66 9766931
www.thesewingshed@
eircom.net
Patchwork and quilting
supplies

Stitch in Time
293 Sandycombe Road
Kew
Surrey TW9 3LU
Tel: 020 8948 8462
www.stitchintimeuk.com
Specialist quilting retailer

Strawberry Fayre
Chagford
Devon TQ13 8EN
Tel: 01647 433250
Mail order fabrics and quilts

Sunflower Fabrics
157-159 Castle Road
Bedford MK40 3RS
Tel: 01234 273819
www.sunflowerfabrics.com
Quilting supplies

Worn and Washed
The Walled Garden
48 East Street
Olney
Bucks MK 46 4DW
Tel: 01234 240881
Email:kim@
wornandwashedfabrics.com

South Africa
Crafty Supplies
Stadium on Main
Main Road
Claremont 7700
Tel: 021 671 0286
Fern Gully
46 3rd Street
Linden
2195
Tel: 011 782 7941

Nimble Fingers
Shop 222
Kloof Village Mall
Village Road
Kloof 3610
Tel: 031 764 6283

Pied Piper
69 1st Avenue
Newton Park
Port Elizabeth 6001
Tel: 041 365 1616

Quilt Talk
40 Victoria Street
George 6530
Tel: 044 873 2947

Quilt Tech
9 Louanna Avenue
Kloofendal
Extension 5 1709
Tel: 011 679 4386

Quilting Supplies
42 Nellnapius Drive
Irene 0062
Tel: 012 667 2223

Simply Stitches
2 Topaz Street
Albernarle
Germiston 1401
Tel: 011 902 6997

Stitch 'n' Stuff
140 Lansdowne Road
Claremont 7700
Tel: 021 674 4059

Australia
Country Patchwork Cottage
10/86 Erindale Road
Balcatta
WA 6021
Tel: (08) 9345 3550

Patchwork of Essendon
96 Fletcher Street
Essendon
VIC 3040
Tel: (03) 9372 0793

Patchwork Plus
Shop 81
7-15 Jackson Avenue
Miranda
NSW 2228
Tel: (02) 9540 278

The Quilters Store
22 Shaw Street
Auchenflower
QLD 4066
Tel: (07) 3870 0408

Quilts and Threads
827 Lower North East Road
Dernancourt
SA 5075
Tel: (08) 8365 6711

Riverlea Cottage Quilts
Shop 4, 330 Unley Road
Hyde Park
SA 5061
Tel: (08) 8373 0653

New Zealand
Grandmothers Garden Patchwork and Quilting
1042 Gordonton Road
Gordonton
Hamilton
Tel: (07) 824 3050

Hands Ashford Craft Supply Store
5 Normans Road
Christchurch
Tel: (03) 355 9099
www.hands.co.nz

Needlecraft Distributors
600 Main Street
Palmerston North
Tel: (06) 356 4793
Fax: (06) 355 4594

Patchwork Barn
132 Hinemoa Street
Birkenhead
Auckland
Tel: (09) 480 5401

The Patchwork Shop
356 Grey Street
Hamilton
Tel: (07) 856 6365

The Quilt Shop
35 Pearn Place
Northcote Shopping Centre
Auckland
Tel: (09) 480 0028
Fax: (09) 480 0380

Spotlight Stores
Whangarei (09) 430 7220
Wairau Park (09) 444 0220
Henderson (09) 836 0888
Panmure (09) 527 0915
Manukau City (09) 263 6760
Hamilton (07) 839 1793
Rotorua (07) 343 6901
New Plymouth (06) 757 3575
Gisborne (06) 863 0037
Hastings (06) 878 5223
Palmerston North (06) 357 6833
Porirua (04) 238 4055
Wellington (04) 472 5600
Christchurch (03) 377 6121
Dunedin (03) 477 1478
www.spotlight.net.nz

Stitch and Craft
32 East Tamaki Road
Papatoetoe
Auckland
Tel: (09) 278 1351
Fax: (09) 278 1356

Stitches
351 Colombo Street
Christchurch
Tel: (03) 379 1868
Fax: (03) 377 2347
www.stitches.co.nz

Variety Handcrafts
106 Princes Street
Dunedin
Tel: (03) 474 1088